A WORLD

UNSUSPECTED

A World

Published for the Center for
Documentary Photography, Duke University,
by the University of North Carolina Press,
Chapel Hill and London

Sheila Bosworth
Robb Forman Dew
Barry Hannah
Josephine Humphreys
James Alan McPherson
Bobbie Ann Mason
T. R. Pearson
Padgett Powell
Dave Smith
Ellease Southerland
Al Young

Unsuspected

*Portraits of
Southern Childhood*

*Edited and with
an introduction by
Alex Harris*

*The Lyndhurst Series
on the South*

This is the first in a series of five books
on the South supported by the
Lyndhurst Foundation of Chattanooga, Tennessee.

Library of Congress Cataloging-in-Publication Data
A World unsuspected.
    (The Lyndhurst series on the South)
    1. Novelists, American—Southern States—Biography—
Youth. 2. Novelists, American—20th century—Biography—
Youth. 3. Children—Southern States. 4. Southern
States—Social life and customs—1865–
5. Photography, Documentary—Southern States.
6. Southern States—Biography. I. Harris, Alex,
1949– . II. Bosworth, Sheila. III. Duke
University. Center for Documentary Photography.
IV. Series.
PS261.W67   1987   813'.54'09975   87-5085
ISBN 0-8078-1748-1

"Introduction" by Alex Harris. Text and
photographs © 1987 Alex Harris.

"My Real Invisible Self" by Josephine
Humphreys. Text and photographs © 1987
Josephine Humphreys.

"Hitting Back" by Padgett Powell. Text and
photographs © 1987 Padgett Powell.

"Didn't Mean Good-bye" by Sheila Bosworth.
Text and photographs © 1987 Sheila
Bosworth.

"Reaching the Stars: My Life as a Fifties
Groupie" by Bobbie Ann Mason. Text and
photographs © 1986, 1987 Bobbie Ann
Mason.

"Going Up to Atlanta" by James Alan
McPherson. Text and photographs © 1986,
1987 James Alan McPherson.

"The Power and the Glory" by Robb Forman
Dew. Text and photographs © 1987 Robb
Forman Dew.

"Unripened Light" by Al Young. Text and
photographs © 1987 Al Young.

"When We Used to Go Where We Went" by
T. R. Pearson. Text and photographs © 1987
T. R. Pearson.

"Your Own Beautiful Lie" by Barry Hannah.
Text and photographs © 1987 Barry Hannah.

"I Got a Horn, You Got a Horn" by Ellease
Southerland. Text and photographs © 1987
Ellease Southerland.

"A Secret You Can't Break Free" by Dave
Smith. Text and photographs © 1986, 1987
Dave Smith.

The editor gratefully acknowledges
permission to reprint an excerpt from Paterson
by William Carlos Williams © 1958 William
Carlos Williams. Reprinted by permission of
New Directions Publishing Corporation.

A portion of "Going Up to Atlanta" by James
Alan McPherson first appeared in Southern
Magazine under the title "A Belief in Electricity."

"Reaching the Stars: My Life as a Fifties
Groupie" by Bobbie Ann Mason first appeared
in the New Yorker. Reprinted by permission of
the New Yorker.

A portion of "A Secret You Can't Break Free"
by Dave Smith first appeared in the
Washington Post Magazine.

Designed by Richard Hendel

The descent beckons
        as the ascent beckoned
                Memory is a kind
of accomplishment
        a sort of renewal
                even
an initiation, since the spaces it opens are new
places
        inhabited by hordes
                heretofore unrealized,
of new kinds—
        since their movements
                are towards new objectives
(even though formerly they were abandoned)

No defeat is made up entirely of defeat—since
the world it opens is always a place
        formerly
                unsuspected. A
world lost,
        a world unsuspected
                beckons to new places

                        William Carlos Williams

CONTENTS

Acknowledgments / ix

Introduction
by Alex Harris / xiii

My Real Invisible Self
by Josephine Humphreys / 1

Hitting Back
by Padgett Powell / 14

Didn't Mean Good-bye
by Sheila Bosworth / 36

Reaching the Stars:
My Life as a Fifties Groupie
by Bobbie Ann Mason / 53

Going Up to Atlanta
by James Alan McPherson / 78

The Power and the Glory
by Robb Forman Dew / 108

Unripened Light
by Al Young / 127

When We Used to Go Where We Went
by T. R. Pearson / 139

Your Own Beautiful Lie
by Barry Hannah / 160

I Got a Horn, You Got a Horn
by Ellease Southerland / 175

A Secret You Can't Break Free
by Dave Smith / 210

Contributors / 235

ACKNOWLEDGMENTS

Of the many people who helped to shape *A World Unsuspected*, I am particularly indebted to Deaderick Montague at the Lyndhurst Foundation in Chattanooga, Tennessee, and Dorothy Abbott at the Center for the Study of Southern Culture at the University of Mississippi, in Oxford, Mississippi. Rick planted the seed for the idea for this book by suggesting a new approach to documentary books and by urging me to look seriously at Southern writers. Few people know Southern writers and Southern writing as well as Dorothy Abbott. Over the last two years, Dottie has unselfishly shared with me both her expert advice and her extensive address book.

In learning about the new generation of fiction writers and determining which books to read, I relied on the counsel of a number of individuals: in Chapel Hill, North Carolina, Max Steele, Iris Tillman Hill, and William de-Buys; in Winston-Salem, North Carolina, John Ehle; in Greensboro, North Carolina, Fred Chappell; in Durham, North Carolina, Reynolds Price, Robert Long of the North Carolina Writers' Network, and John Valentine of Regulator Books; in Charleston, South Carolina, Pete and Connie Wyrick, Nan Morrison, Daniel Fort, and the staff of the First Edition Bookstore; in Oxford, Mississippi, William Ferris. At various stages of this project I also received important recommendations on writers and on the structure of this book from Peter Decker, Peggy Prenshaw, Ted Rosengarten, Carol Stack, Mary Williams, Gus Blaisdell, Toni Morrison, Charles Rowell, Claudia Tate, Henry Louis Gates, and Mary Helen Washington.

Since 1980 I have been very fortunate to work closely with the editors and staff of the University of North Carolina Press. I originally came to UNC Press because of the brilliant design work of Richard Hendel and continue to be grateful for his advice and fine work. Iris Tillman Hill nurtured the idea for this book and helped to steer the project from the beginning. I am grateful to Matthew Hodgson for his counsel and encouragement. I also want to

x

Acknowledgments

single out Johanna Grimes and Paul Betz for their dedicated work on this book.

At Duke University, I would like to thank my colleagues at the Institute of Policy Sciences and Public Affairs for their continued support of my work at the Center for Documentary Photography.

For reading and commenting on my introduction to this book, I want to thank: William deBuys, Daniel Voll, Roger Rawlings, Bobbie Ann Mason, Peter Decker, Robb Forman Dew, Ellease Southerland, Padgett Powell, John Moses, and Robert Coles. Any failures in the piece are mine not theirs. Throughout this project, I have relied on the advice of the individual writers in this book. The opportunity to come to know a number of these Southern writers has been the real pleasure of this project.

This book exists primarily through the generosity of the Lyndhurst Foundation. I want to thank Deaderick Montague, Jack Murrah, and Eleanor Cooper of Lyndhurst for their confidence in me as the general editor of this first in a series of documentary books on the South. I am especially grateful for the award I received from the Lyndhurst Foundation in 1984, giving me the sanction and time to pursue this book and my own photographic work.

I am grateful to my father, Arthur Harris, for instilling in me a love for books, an appreciation that provided much of the inspiration for this project. I want to thank my sister, Jill Harris Brown, for her help over the last year with some of our family photographs in this book. Though I am listed as the editor of this book, my wife, Margaret Sartor, has generously shared her ideas with me over the last two years and deserves credit for much of the concept of the project. Once again, I want to single out Robert Coles both for the example of his work as well as for the encouragement and advice he has given on this book.

A. H.

To the Memory of Alexander Eisemann, 1888–1953

INTRODUCTION

ALEX HARRIS

I remember a small antique table in our living room. It was shaped like a baby carriage with legs, an elaborate wooden basket of dark, oiled, and inlaid mahogany with a canopy in back made from another dark wood. Underneath this canopy were several vertical compartments which held our family photograph albums. Over thirty years ago as a child of six growing up in Atlanta, Georgia, I had just learned the story of Moses in the ark of bulrushes and this oddly shaped table always made me think of the baby Moses floating down the Nile alone.

Next to that table stood a couch, and if I climbed up on the couch and leaned over the table I could just manage to lift out the albums—one by one. I don't remember the exact day I discovered all this, but I know that once I found those picture albums I went back to that spot again and again to pore over a world created by my maternal grandfather, an amateur photographer with a passion for recording moments in the lives of his two children, and later his grandchildren.

One of the albums with a red leather cover was devoted solely to my mother from early childhood to courting days, and it fascinated me and frankly made me more than a little jealous to see her there before I was even born having such a good time. But the album I spent the most hours gazing at was the brown one about my brother, my sister, and me.

There was something so solid and reassuring about those pages of pictures where we were always together, posing proudly for the camera or lost in the games of our own invention. No matter what seemed strange or scary in my day-to-day life, I could count on the constancy of my grandfather's brown book. He had chosen to preserve some of our best moments for us, and sequenced and arranged these with affection and care. Every picture was

Artie, Alex, and Jill Harris. Atlanta, Georgia, 1952.

neatly dated and captioned in his slanted longhand, often with poems or funny stories scribbled into the margins. And in the bottom righthand corner of his snapshots, my grandfather often embossed this phrase: "Candid Camera Greetings—Alex Eisemann." For me, it was as if that moment had been officially approved and sanctioned.

Over the months, as I looked at those pictures, I began to do something that until a few years ago had always seemed at best odd and confusing, at worst the beginning of a mental illness that would surely overwhelm me in old age. I began to make up my own stories about those pictures and the life of my family, fictions conceived in such elaborate detail that it is now difficult for me to remember what was real and what was fantasy, what I lived and what I dreamed.

The writers of this volume of stories were given the challenge of making a distinction between that world of dreams and the life they have actually lived, of stepping away from the freedom of fiction to the constraints of the nonfiction genre. In an assignment any first-year psychiatry resident would see as an acute form of "acting-out" behavior by one very industrious editor, I asked these writers to look at their own family photograph albums, and using these snapshots as a catalyst for memory, to tell the *true* story of their childhoods. I was really asking for a clearer sense of my own past, but in the end each writer returned to me what Dave Smith calls "a secret you can't break free," what Barry Hannah labels "your own beautiful lie." In the end I understood that memories are stories we tell ourselves, and like the stories in this book, like the history of the South, memories have to do with the imagination.

In 1984 I began reading novels. Of course I had read novels before, but in 1984 I began reading novels in earnest. Like Binx Bolling in Walker Percy's *The Moviegoer*, I was on to something, and I read to the exclusion of practically all other activities. This was no ordinary existential search.

At Duke University's Center for Documentary Photography, we had received that year a grant from the Lyndhurst Foundation to publish a series of five books on the South, of which this book is now the first. Our books were to be in the distinguished tradition of the University of North Carolina Press documentary publications that came out of the South in the 1920s and 1930s, the time of the Southern literary renaissance. Those were books by scholars like Howard Odum and Rupert Vance who wrote clearly and compassionately about the human problems of the South, and by implication, about the problems of our nation in the early twentieth century. Those documentary books were experimental. They went beyond the accepted limits of social science and helped to form and define a new kind of documentary writing, a definition we hoped in our new series to expand and refine.

The Foundation put only one significant stipulation on the grant we received: that in each book we give at least equal weight to writing as to photography. I had come to know a number of the South's finest photographers, and had read the work of older generations of distinguished Southern novelists, the likes of Welty, Warren, Percy, and Price; so I turned first to research what I knew least—the writers of my own generation in the South, those born around 1940 or later, growing up in the postwar era.

Clearly these were novelists and short story writers already well versed in photography—not in the photographic process, but in the process of using photographs to help describe the world. The original idea for this book came to me one day in Durham, while reading Bobbie Ann Mason's *Shiloh and Other Stories*. Photographs and photographers showed up again and again in her pages, sometimes emerging quite literally from the woodwork. Mason used pictures in her fiction as a way to illuminate a story, to evoke memories in her characters. Then late one night in Charleston, reading Josephine Humphreys's *Dreams of Sleep*, I realized as well how a writer could use a photograph to confound memory, to deepen the mystery of a story.

It occurred to me that for the first book in our series I would ask a number of the South's best storytellers to continue what they were already doing, to look at pictures as a way to facilitate telling their stories; but in this case, the images would be from their own family photo albums. If I could find a diverse enough group of young writers, their stories might come to represent the experiences of a whole generation growing up in the South.

I began to correspond with a number of Southern novelists and short story writers, over twenty in all, in hopes that I could find a group willing to take on this project. Some declined, but for all who accepted, the assignment was the same: to make their family snapshots a starting point for writing down some of their childhood memories.

The writers were free to take their own distinctive approaches to the project. They could recount one episode in a childhood or cover a broad range of time; their stories could be "short-story length." I made it clear that image quality should not be a factor in their choice of pictures. All the better if their snapshots resembled the seemingly ordinary photographs in most of our family albums. Even the number of pictures was not prescribed. After all, Harry Crews had written at length in *A Childhood* about the father he never knew, using only one crumpled snapshot for his inspiration. The pictures were to be seen as catalysts for memory, as stimulation for stories, not an end in themselves.

This first book in our series on the South is not an anthology. The stories were not selected. The writing is different, richer, more resonant than I could have planned or chosen, than the writers themselves could have foreseen. With this book, we move away from a traditional format of documentary publication in which a photographer looks at the world and a writer explains what the photographer sees. At the Center for Documentary Photography we will continue to explore different ways of combining visual and verbal language for our series. We will follow the lead of the writers in this book in using one language to inspire the other, to augment the power of the other. We will follow the lead of the writers in this book by taking chances. We want to make each book an act of exploration.

This book is part of a broad and diverse documentary tradition, and in fact flows directly from the pioneering work of oral historians who since the

1940s have used what they call "material culture" to generate stories, to help find significance in a particular life or historical period. These historians have gone beyond what in conventional social science is considered a "primary" source—the first written eyewitness account of a historical event—to speak with the individuals who have lived through a particular time, to consider and preserve their stories. The documentary tradition embraces the work of historians who, like Theodore Rosengarten in *All God's Dangers*, have turned to stories from everyday life, to the Nate Shaws of the world, like the writers in this book, to the best storytellers they can find.

We are most familiar with documentary work of photographers and film-makers fighting for social change, urging others to learn, to understand—to feel the experiences of individuals they might not otherwise come to know. But documentary unites a huge body of material, is defined by a number of means of expression, because documentary is not a type of research, not a genre. Documentary is an approach.

Documentarians learn about the world by participating in it. They look and listen and record. They are not trying to construct a theory; instead they want to render. They immerse themselves in particular communities in hopes of getting to know individuals, people viewed not as subjects, but as colleagues, as teachers, as friends to whom one appeals for information and help.

The stories in this book seem to me to lie at the heart of the documentary tradition—in exploring the truth about the subjective world, in uncovering what William Stott calls "the facts of feelings." But documentary is never purely narcissistic. Its focus can be inward, but at its best, documentary makes the connection between the interior and exterior world.

Surely fiction is documentary whenever writers come close to the truth about the way real people feel about their lives and experiences. Poetry is documentary when it celebrates the beauty of what people say and how they say it. The blues is documentary in coming to terms with what is lost to the singer and to all of us, and as with storytelling, in the pleasure of the singing and the telling and the listening.

Even the work of many physicians can be considered documentary work —not just the work of the poet/physician William Carlos Williams, or the playwright/physician Anton Chekov, or the novelist/physician Walker Percy, or, for lack of a more precise characterization, the writer/physician Robert Coles. Medicine has incorporated the documentary approach since Hippocrates urged the physicians who followed him to attempt to know the whole person in all aspects of being: from environment to diet, from emotions to physical symptoms—in short, to have contact with society and to observe human nature.

The impulse to observe and document human nature is a part of all our lives. We try to describe and validate our experience of the world, prove we are here . . . were there. In our diaries and photo albums we turn, as my grandfather did, to make a record of personal and family history. In the South, it is not uncommon for young women to keep a private album of snapshots and other memorabilia until they marry. In my wife's family there are three generations of such books, her own, her mother's and her grand-mother's, all documenting the life of the same town in northern Louisiana.

This book owes much to the work of the distinguished American photographer Walker Evans, who was so often labeled a documentary photographer though he didn't like the term as it was narrowly defined during much of his lifetime. In the 1930s, the camera was considered the ideal tool for documentary, for communicating the unadulterated truth about the physical world. But Evans knew that the camera takes on the personality of the holder, that "the mind works on the machine, or through it." With his seemingly dispassionate eye and straightforward style, Walker Evans might appear an odd influence for a book of childhood memories and family snapshots. Yet like the writers in this book, he was essentially interested in time and the effects of time.

In 1970 at Evans's house in Connecticut, I first saw a photograph he had made in the summer of 1936 of tenant family snapshots tacked to a rough-sawn Alabama cabin wall, and another startling photograph of dozens of professional portraits displayed together in the window of a Savannah, Georgia, photography studio, circa 1935. Evans was looking at what he called the "vernacular," but he seemed to be saying in his ironic yet utterly believable way, "If you want to know a people, then this is evidence you should consider."

We tend to believe the content of a snapshot or a portrait that looks like a snapshot before we believe more accomplished photographic art. As much as anything else, the unselfconscious style of Eudora Welty's Depression-era photographs makes them appear to ring so true, oddly enough, with an approach and ultimate meaning in direct opposition to most of the accepted and acclaimed work of the Farm Security Administration photographers of the same era. Robert Frank in the 1950s, and later Emmet Gowin, Gary Winogrand, Lee Friedlander, and many other professional photographers, understood the power of the vernacular when they worked and played with a snapshot aesthetic.

My real understanding of the power of the vernacular came from a group of amateur photographers. Like the people who made the photographs in this book, these photographers were making a record for themselves and their families. Like Eudora Welty in Mississippi, they were part of the world they documented and moved freely within it.

I began to grasp the power of the vernacular in 1973, when I made a trip to a remote Alaskan Eskimo village above the Arctic Circle. For me, this was the beginning of a photographic study of the life of these isolated villages, a project I pursued intermittently over a period of six years. From the start, the Eskimos I met and lived with were open to and fully participated in the act of being photographed. In fact, each Eskimo home had its own family snapshot album, many of the pictures dating back to cameras the Eskimos borrowed from the first missionaries at the turn of the century. Thinking I was doing the Eskimos a favor, I began to copy many of the oldest snapshots, some of which were literally crumbling, and on a return trip to that village, gave back new, enlarged copies to each family.

After my first couple of trips to Alaska, I began to study those copies of Eskimo snapshots at home in North Carolina and compare them to the pictures I was making. In my photographs the Eskimos seemed a close-knit people, proud, hardworking, almost stoic in the face of a difficult life. But in the Eskimos' family snapshots, there was so much humor, such laughter and outright joy, that I started to question my own work, the vision I seemed to be imposing on this people.

On the one hand, I knew that in my photographs I was trying to be true to life as I saw and experienced it, and moreover that my pictures were appreciated and admired by the Eskimos themselves. On the other hand, it was clear that something was missing, that I had been unconsciously editing certain kinds of moments, portraying these people in too narrow a way. On subsequent trips to the villages, I looked for, found, and later photographed what I had been ignoring—some of those joyful moments in the lives of Eskimo families. When the time came to publish my work in a book, I included a section of Eskimo snapshots, and explained how these pictures had influenced me.

A World Unsuspected seems to me now a further exploration of the experience of learning from snapshots, of looking at the past and finding in a photograph the key to something missing, forgotten, or ignored, of seeing an image and gaining perspective, retrospective, of using a picture for reflection, to help throw light on the mystery of memory, which in the end was the mystery these eleven Southern writers were asked to explore. *A World Unsuspected* provides these fiction writers another kind of opportunity to take their place within the documentary tradition: to translate, record, distill, even embroider—to help create our collective memory. We have always looked to a special few to give meaning to our common experience, to carry forth from the past something we haven't seen, could never have seen without first being shown, and having been shown could never see again without knowing, without remembering.

We may someday be able to dissect the anatomy of the mind, comprehend from science the precise way thoughts and feelings are formed, stored, and recalled, understand the exact location in the brain, the very enzymes and neurons, the narrow path of synapses that fire—to make a memory. But I do not believe we will know more about memory than we are shown in this book by our short story writers and novelists, by our writers of fiction. I do not believe we will know more than William Faulkner showed us back in 1932 in *Light in August* when he wrote: "Memory believes before knowing remembers. Believes longer than recollects, longer than knowing even wonders."

A WORLD

UNSUSPECTED

MY REAL

INVISIBLE

SELF

JOSEPHINE HUMPHREYS

*E*very year we line up a new photographer. My grandmother, Neta, looks in the Yellow Pages, hoping to find the same one we had for last year's Christmas picture. But last year's man is never there.

"They get run out of town," I say from her four-poster bed. When my parents are at work, we laze around the house. Neta lets me and my sisters put on dresses left over from her better days. I lie in bed wearing a chiffon with silk rosettes at the shoulder. I smoke Neta's Viceroys. Because of her great love for me, she is in my power, indulgent as a man charmed by a new woman.

She looks at me. "Artists are often itinerant," she says.

I make a mental note of "itinerant." Most of my vocabulary has come from Neta, who talks to me as if I'm a real person rather than a thirteen-year-old. We are more than grandmother and granddaughter; we fascinate and educate each other. There are things she wants me to know, but she does not come out and say them. I am to watch and listen and put two and two together.

"You love those photographers," I say. This is an accusation. I talk sassy to her because I am desperate to keep her.

"They have their appeal," she says absently. It is hard to converse with a woman who often seems to be talking to herself. Her mind is off and running. Mine scrambles to keep up.

Seasons Greetings
from our house to your house

Wm, Martha, Josephine, Kiki

Wishing you a merry Christmas from

"The Girls"   Neta

Josephine Humphreys

She came as a sixteen-year-old bride to South Carolina from Texas. With her black hair and big nose she looks like a Navajo. Church Street in Charleston is not a place where you would expect to find a woman like this (you would look in Paris or in Taos), but she was stranded here by divorce. In the thirties, there were only a couple of grounds you could divorce on. Her husband, who' had run into somebody he liked better, got doctors' signatures and obtained the divorce on the grounds of craziness. He let her keep the house—where my parents and my sisters and I live with her—and her piano, her bed, her beautiful clothes.

I know why she likes the photographers. They are a certain type, the wandering type, the disconnected type. She calls them artists. I tell her that my personal opinion of them is low; they are not artists but misfits. I say it is disgusting to have my picture taken by a man whose lip sweats and who has spots on his face. This man is not in photography for art's sake; he is in it because he can't make small talk or tell a joke or sell an insurance policy. When I say this, Neta says, "Well, yes, perhaps you're right." Then she looks at me; she studies me.

I am possessed by orneriness. At the moment it is the only way to keep her attention. I have seen women turn ornery on men, balk and carp, because what else can they do? Neta is day-dreamy lately. If I don't engage her attention, it will disconnect.

She sits on the side of the bed and holds the phone book with its spine dropped down between her knees, its pages open like unfolded wings across her legs.

She mails a hundred cards. I can't figure out where she gets a hundred people to mail cards to; I thought we were her only friends. When I ask, she says she mails them to former acquaintances to prove she is alive and kicking. Sometimes across the face of the card she writes a breezy message, like "Wishing you happiness in the coming year."

Sometimes she will take all the past cards and fan them out like a canasta hand and deal them onto the table, the accumulated history of our childhood. The total effect is impressive, a sense of continued well-being in a family, normal growth occurring. But to be honest, the pictures show us as happier than I remember us being. I am surprised when I see them all together, amazed at what the pictures do not show. In reality we bicker, we are grouchy and impatient. But in the pictures we often show up cheery. Even I, who am meanest, appear to be potentially kind and open-hearted. Because of this discrepancy between what the pictures suggest and what I know of us, I have come to doubt the validity of photography as historical record. Instead, it occurs to me that these pictures tell our fortune. They reveal something that is normally not visible: how the future lies curled and hidden in the present. It may be that we ourselves have a good chance at the future happiness our cards wish others. These pictures predict it, in spite of my current despair.

Of Neta's better days, only two photographs remain. One is of her, taken by a society photographer back when she was rich and married. This photograph does not predict happiness. I can see in the remarkable eyes and mouth the bad years coming, even though the picture was taken long before her trouble actually erupted. But there it is. Anyone can see it, in the picture; but perhaps it wasn't visible in real life.

The second surviving photograph is one I found in a hatbox under a red felt hat. I left it there because that is as good a hiding place as any; she never goes through her old clothes. Now and then I look at this picture. It is only a snapshot of a man on a beach, holding a fish. He is proud of the fish. This is a trophy picture, nothing more, an ordinary scrapbook photo fading toward the top. And yet something in it horrifies me: the fish. The fish is enormous, bigger than any I've ever seen. The man's whole torso bends toward the fish, to hold it up. He is not a burly man. In fact, his legs look spindly, to my surprise. But there is power in the arms. He has *got* that fish.

I have never seen the man himself, in person, in real life; and because of the serious attitude toward family rifts in the South, I will never see him. He is prominent, maybe even famous, but as far as I am concerned he exists only in the fish picture, and in the stories I make up to accompany it. The picture is all I have to go on, so each detail of it figures in the stories. I make him a villain every time.

It does not escape my thirteen-year-old eye that his feet are hidden. He stands in the shallow water, and his feet are completely concealed, a significant detail.

Neta runs a red fingernail down the page of numbers. "This name sounds familiar," she says. "Cale Prosser. Have we had him before? Slope-shouldered man, wore a brown suit that shimmered?"

"Cale Prosser, hmm," I say. "He was the man the police had a shootout with last year after he holed up in a beach bungalow and threatened to kill his girlfriend's baby. Could be he's out on parole and taking pictures now."

"Stop it," she says, dialing, smiling.

It's already November, and she is only now putting this call through. She has made no plans for props or theme or costumes. When I hear her talking to Prosser on the phone, I can tell from her voice that she is not all that excited about this year's Christmas card. I lift myself onto an elbow in order to see the expression on her face, but when she hangs up she does not turn toward me. She says, "It's set. Friday." But she is facing the window, and I can't see her eyes.

"I do not want my picture taken," I say, and I wait for her to deny what I suspect—a change in my looks. In the Christmas photos so far, we have been pretty enough. Now my sisters are still pretty, but I have begun to resemble a pony. My face has lengthened. Braces have been put on my teeth to rein them in. My eyes have started to look strange, rolling up until the iris is half under the lid and I look passed-out. My gums show when I smile. The thought has struck me that Neta's lack of enthusiasm for this year's photography has something to do with my looks.

She turns to me, saying nothing, only looking hard. I hope she sees: my main goal in life is to make up for the difficulty she has had in hers. I am the compensation. The trouble is that I myself am not quite enough. She needs an artist, and I am afraid I am only a regular person.

My music career was cut short by the piano teacher, who said she could not in good faith continue to take Neta's money. So Neta signed me up for ballet and tap. We bought the necessary leotards and shoes. But I was not a dancer. Though I could do the five stationary positions, I could not do the pliés and the jetés; not in public. I did not want to call attention to myself in that physical way. As for tap, I could only watch in horror as the other girls leaned forward, whirled their arms in circles, shuffled their bow-tied shoes.

Neta tried to teach me to paint, maybe thinking she knew me well enough to unleash creative powers others had failed to touch. But now she says it is probably too early to know what form my vision will take. We can wait and see, she says.

I believe she is beginning to lose interest in me.

Because of the annual picture-taking in this family, I have come to regard my own childhood with a strange detachment, almost as if it belonged to someone else. I think of it as an interesting story, distinct somehow from my real invisible self. That girl-self is lonesome, dark and ornery, while the story shown in pictures looks bright, charged with possibilities. Three sisters, their hard-working parents, the solitary and mysterious grandmother; the odd town where Christmas is warm and a black man drives buggyloads of Northerners around, where a granddaughter lives thirteen years without laying eyes on the possibly evil grandfather . . . This childhood is full of drama. I tell it to myself in various versions involving betrayal, reunion, and sometimes (but sometimes not) final happiness.

Prosser arrives. Definitely, he is not the man we had last year. He is perhaps the worst we have ever had, a grease-haired man with bags under his eyes, and dirty hands. I think at first that Neta should not even let him into the house, much less take our picture. But she lets him in. She brings him a glass of bourbon, as if she knew his preference without even asking.

I am angry because I've had to do all the planning for this picture. On my own I wrapped empty boxes in Christmas paper so we could appear to be opening gifts. Now I try to arrange my sisters in a good pose, but they are horsing around. One of them has insisted on wearing a skirt and sweater I said she could not wear, decorated with kittens. I do not want to be photographed with those kittens, because this is serious. The theme is Christmas morning. Kittens have nothing to do with it.

"You look absurd," I say.

"Look what I got for Christmas," she squeals. "Nothing!"

"Don't open the box all the way, nutbrain; you're only supposed to partially open it. I told you not to wear those kittens. Your children will look at this picture twenty years from now and ridicule you."

"My children?" She is eleven. The concept of posterity has not developed in her mind. "This is my favorite outfit," she says.

Neta settles into her chair behind the photographer. Usually she sits there and makes suggestions, as if she were a movie director.

"But this isn't a cat picture," I say. "This is a gift-opening scene."

"I have an idea," Neta says, rising from her place. She leaves the room.

Prosser sighs, shifts his weight from one leg to the other, and shoves a plate into the camera. Alone with him we don't speak. He stares at the rug and makes a noise with his teeth that raises the hair on the back of my neck. The man is pitiful; he does not even know how to make conversation with children.

When Neta comes back, she is carrying Roy the cat, who is my age, oozy and scarred from fights, the most unattractive cat in the world. Neta sets him on a damask chair behind us, so that he will be in the photograph. And I was hoping she'd gone for decent clothes for my sister. Instead, cats are the new theme. Neta winks at me.

Oh, I am tired of trying to interpret this woman. It is exhausting to love her; she is always just out of reach, baffling me. It is as easy to believe that she cares nothing for me as to believe that I am all she cares for. In this matter of the cat, which perhaps has no significance, I suspect treachery and the end of love.

"I have another idea," she says. I have given up; if she wants me to cuddle the cat, I will do it. My spirit is broken.

"I want you to write some stories for me," she says, nodding. "Why didn't I think of it before?" In her excitement she lights a cigarette and takes a long drag and never moves her eyes off my face. And once again, she has thrown me for a loop.

Still watching me, she leans close to Prosser, whispering, "No, not yet. Wait. There, yes, now," and he shoots.

My dense and sullen heart lifts at the suggestion, *Write some stories for me.* I have stories ready to go, I have been making them up for years! And I have, as I will later discover, a quality that serves writers well: self-doubt so deep it

is indistinguishable from vanity. Neta saw it and nurtured it. She taught me to look at pictures of myself as if the person there were mysterious and significant.

     After the photography is done, she leads Prosser out onto the porch. Wearing sandals and a full skirt, she looks much younger than any grandmother I have ever seen. She walks young, with an easy, sprung step; and the way she smokes, with her fingers held stiff in a vee, is not sophisticated, but innocent-looking, like a girl with her first cigarette. She and Prosser sit in rocking chairs and smoke and drink bourbon in the warm November afternoon. Through the window in the dining room I have a good view of them, and of the sky between this house and the next. Light comes down yellow and thin as if into a canyon. A line of cormorants crosses the strip of sky. Neta and the photographer drink together with the grace of old friends. Her feet are on the railing, her chair rocked back and cocked.

For the waste of beauty, I despise my grandfather.

I do understand that he was not an evil man; was maybe even a normal enough fellow, a fisherman, cigar-smoker, bit of a gallivanter but able to make small talk and money. And then, she may have been a hard woman to be married to, hungry as she was for something that was not exactly the man himself but only lodged in the man. She might have done with him as she did with me, put the burden of love all on him, until he finally got out from under it. I do try to give him the benefit of the doubt.

But I come back, always, to that snapshot. To that fish. Once, of course, it swam in the sea.

When the sun gets low, Prosser takes his leave, handing over the empty glass. He hangs his camera and his lights and meters from his shoulder and is ready to go, but stops at the door until she comes to him. She takes his hand. What does she see in him? I think it is the same thing she sees in me, the thing she loves in everyone who has it: loneliness. As Prosser backs out the door, I can understand the sweet nature of loneliness; my own breaks open like a seed and shows its rich heart. There is nothing in our lives—his, hers, mine—that needs compensation.

When she took the picture (for surely she was the photographer, that day on the beach) she must have seen in the arms, the cigar, the weight of the hanging bass what was predicted there. She may very well in the click of the shutter have chosen loneliness over endless married life.

The cat card was not the last of the Christmas cards, but it was the last directed by Neta. She was beginning to be sick with the long illness that would go from emphysema to cancer and kill her early. Our final photograph was taken in a shopping-center studio. The picture is sharp, very slick, and completely different from the earlier pictures. You can tell when you look at it that Neta is not there, behind the camera, looking for our best angle. Neta is not there, seeing us.

HITTING

BACK

PADGETT POWELL

O ne's personal history, it seems dangerously obvious to me, is ordered precisely as a drawer of family snapshots:
it is *not* ordered, it is lost, it is illogically duplicate (there are several copies of
insignificant photos, while dear ones are absent—one lives dull days again
and again, while the big moments go forever underexposed), it is finally
random. To recount a history, you open a drawer. You find twenty-five-year-
old 2″x4″ Smithsonian-grade black-and-whites somehow on top of last year's
lousy instant Polaroids. You discover packets of orange negatives melted together which could yet be developed into public prints.

I think there are these orange negatives in our histories, in our heads. Take
the photo of me with my harem, circa 1957. Many things are set, by this age,
in that emulsion which is soon to be called one's character, and these elements and forces are readable in the photographic emulsion before us. Note
my girls. Whether they have been perversely grouped like this by an adult,
or whether they adore me truly, or whether I have engineered the scene
myself (surely the running-board leg is my own touch), they are indubitably
mine, possessed as fully as a good bigamist may possess them on the occasion of his fifth birthday. My chief wife is the girl at front, the tallest and the
blondest, qualities which presumably suggested to me at the time the wom-
anly equivalent of Forrest's fustest and mostest. She got there first with the
most to my early reckoning, and ever since, my chief wife—filtered from the
venereal welter of short gropings that gets us to our longer mates—my chief
wives have been tall and they have been blond.

My leg is up on the running board: I am, in putting it up, putting my foot *down*, taking presumptuous charge of the situation and of all these admirers. It is the same today. Arbitrary, foolish, with a streak of petulance and defiance, finally confident, what is implicit in this snapshot at five is extant at thirty-five.

This is a halcyon time. The nursery school in Tallahassee, Florida, where this is taken is run by a woman named Mrs. Apthorp, and her son, who is in the Army, comes home on leave and does two things which delight us: he perforates the grounds with practice foxholes, and he spreads a giant canvas tarp over an entire mimosa tree. We spend days collecting the amber, rubbery gum from now unidentifiable trees, and regard it as a kind of tribal currency (we call it goulash), poking it and handling it and bartering it in the gloom and waterproofed air beneath the living tent.

There are two shots contemporary to this one that were not taken except in the orange emulsion of my head. I will submit that they are nonetheless as telling, as durable, as this found photo. The halcyon days at Mrs. Apthorp's do not last forever (Could they? Does the scene somehow not prefigure Warren Beatty and Faye Dunaway in their doomed gangster love?), and I matriculate at kindergarten. There I begin becoming a racist, a queer and squir-

relly kind of racist, but one all the same, and probably not one less dangerous than the normal kind. This new school does not have the Club Med
glamour and ease of Mrs. Apthorp's; we are in a meaner bourgeois affair with
hired help about (at Mrs. Apthorp's you dealt with Mrs. Apthorp). One of
these functionaries is a woman who works in the kitchen: that is to say, she
opens and heats the #10 cans of Chef Boy-ar-dee and serves it on pastel
plastic plates with compartments. She also personally attends to her nephew,
a little pen-raised bastard who has not, by age four or five, learned the use of
a fork. His specially large portions of Boy-ar-dee are rammed, snatched,
smeared onto his pasty face with an abandon that claims half the dining area.
The aunt stands protectively by, spoon and pot at the ready to reload little
Gary.

At this point, I have nothing against little Gary, though I do wish he would
train to fork. There he is, with the thin, gelatinous sauce of Boy-ar-dee all
over him, several broken pieces of pasta plastered, annealed, to his face in
the orange glue—big fat cheap soft busted spaghetti resembling maggots.
And there is his aunt, moving as nimbly as can a two- to three-hundred-
pound woman with a ten-gallon stainless pot on her hip and a large serving
spoon in the air, Gary barking *More! More!* I have nothing against little Gary
and his aunt, and it is debatable whether I understand, or even apprehend,
at age five, the term *underbred*.

It comes Halloween. I get up as a pirate. My mother is an accomplished
costumer and does me up for years in stage-grade disguises. In the sixth
grade she will get me up in drag—basic black and pearl choker, C-cup wash-
cloth tits—and I perversely will go out *in the afternoon* for a round of solo
trick-or-treating. I transfixed a man, *froze* a man, who could not close his
front door as I swiveled away down his driveway, giving him a little Marilyn
kiss over the shoulder. Sometime later, I heard that this fellow hung himself
in his garage, and felt the smallest tremor of complicity. There is no photo of
this Natalie Wood costume, or of the pirate costume in question; suffice the
Indian.

As a good pirate then, with eye-patch and short sword, I walk in on little
Gary, who is on the toilet about the business of "making grunt" of his Boy-ar-
dee. "Little Gary is in there making grunt," his aunt says in my fictive universe today, when I *do* have something against the underbred.

Well, Gary, before I can apologize for the intrusion or even back out, runs
hobbled by his pants out of the bathroom. I proceed with my business,

whether making grunt or tinkling I do not recall. I manage neither operation
before the mustachioed aunt crashes in, accusing me of deliberately scaring
Gary, and sits me down against a wall, and commands that I remain there. I
tell her the costume scared him, that I just—she will hear none of it. She
leaves me there until, it seems, I am rescued by some other, higher function-
ary, but it is a long time I am against that wall becoming aware, for damned
sure, that some people are not good people. I do not know when in one's
career as a not-Christian one begins to use the term *white trash*, but I know
that once I had the concept I had no trouble filing Gary and his aunt as my
very first specimens.

Now, take the photo of me, my mother, and a beagle named Gyp. We are yet in Tallahassee. An interesting thing happens one day in this yard. There is no photo of it. That there is no photo tells more than if there were. This yard is cared for by a colored man, a term I will use for its historical accuracy. I recall him vaguely: khaki pants, easy moves, keeping quiet. One day, upon some odd occasion that I got into a conversation with him, I did two things in the presence of my mother which represented the very cornerstones of the good manners my parents were insistent one display: I addressed the yard-man as *Mister*, and I responded to him *Yes, sir*. These are two simple but powerful tools one can use even today with startling good results, and I am fond of using them when in the presence of elders who regard the world as one of irremediable decline, and I might even have been selfishly expecting some subtle profit to come from so addressing a yardman in 1957. But only moments after this exchange I was told by my mother that the *Mr.* and the *sir* were not correct. At this abrogation of absolutes I can honestly report being mystified: Why not? You just don't.

My mother put this to me gently, and, I would like to suggest, a bit sadly, for I believe we are not bigoted in any vigorous way but in the way of simple, inertial, white *status quo*. And I think the *status-quo* saddle would have been

an altogether comfortable one for me to ride if I had not been frightened into peeing in my pants by a three-hundred-pound mustachioed harridan protecting her fyce nephew to whom (her, not grunting Gary) I *did* have to say *Yes, ma'am.* And that same inculcated respect for elders commanded that I obey that monster and sit against that wall in a pirate suit, a respect undone for a silent, hard-working man in the sun with a worn-out, wobbly-wheeled lawn mower. It may be a sleight of fancy to yoke these two moments into a sequential one-two of character-developing meaning, but I will: when I could not say *sir* to the yardman, and when I had to sit against the wall for a shrew-blind white slob, I became a racist—reverse, whip, anti-, obverse, perverse, any way you want to term it. It occurs to me now that I have another story not unlike this one—following the same racial parameters and the same behavioral patterns revealed in this one. I will try to work back to it. First, another party shot.

I am again impressed with the way these photos seem to contain, or telegraph, later character, as was suggested a bit speciously (perhaps) regarding one's lasting nursery-school taste in women. In the party shot, of the same era, note the sailor-suited boy who appears particularly disapproving as the rest of us party down. He has gone on to live something of a troubled life, I hear. And I to something more like a well-adjusted partying life. There is a longer story in this picture which will yet develop the matter of respect for folk, showing it and claiming it.

Sitting on a swing, I am wearing one of my favorite suits—I will be well dressed until college, when my mother can no longer coordinate and set out my clothes so that I don't wear anything that "clashes." As, indeed, she has done here. One day, wearing this natty outfit or one like it, I had been playing with my disapproving friend, and after play, inside, discovered *dog shit* in the pocket of this handsome blouse. What was particularly galling was my mistaking the matter for dirt until virtually tasting it in the course of my assay. I concluded that my friend Don had put the shit in my shirt: it must have slid off the hoe when he hit me in the head with the hoe. That—being struck—was regular and acceptable. But this fouling of one's wardrobe was a bit wide of beam, perhaps even my mother was besmirched, and I recall this moment as my very first instant of moral outrage. I did nothing about it.

I did nothing about it until my father did something about it, and it wasn't the shit in my pocket that motivated him, it was the screaming. My friend, as I say, was accustomed to hitting me, unprovoked, and I would repair home crying. Some time shortly after the fouled-pocket affair, I received a particularly gratuitous, open-palmed slap to the center of my back, and ran into the house wailing, a virtual emergency siren. My father grabbed me and told me I need not worry so much anymore about Don hitting me, because if he did it again, and I did not hit back, *he* would hit me. He was a belt man, and fast. I considered his promise, knew it to be genuine, and calculated that I'd be wasting time if I waited for Don to strike again. And who knew: the next blow might overwhelm me into another defenseless retreat, while I had the present affront assimilated. Emboldened by the larger fear of my father, giddy to discover it correct to clobber someone, perhaps shamed by the pure discovery that in being polite I had been apparently cowardly, and not unmindful of my nice yellow suit top with its pen pocket recently full of shit, I went to Don's house next door, stopping a moment in our carport for a tool.

I asked to see Don. Don presented himself on the screen porch, opened the door, I grabbed his arm and jerked him out, down, and across the concrete steps, and began to whale away approximately at the small of his back with a claw hammer. His mother pulled me off before I could seriously hurt him. It worked. Don never struck me again, and we spent another off-and-on ten years together.

My father told me this magical I'll-hit-you formula three times. I am afraid it worked only this first time, if assault with a deadly weapon can be construed a workable solution (I think it can). The second time was during my first at-bat in my first Little League ball game. I was on a team of scrubs, a consolation team made up of boys too young or small or crummy to be on a competitive team (they named us the Mullets and let other teams practice on us, though as I recall only one team ever played us, rather like the Globetrotters and their dummy opponents). At the plate, I discovered I had a natural move to the bucket: you move your rear leg back and away from the plate, which (1) takes you out of hitting range and (2) indicates scared batter. Deep, then, in the bucket, I watched two perfect strikes zip by and was bodily lifted from the batter's box by my father. He applied the formula: "If you step in the bucket one more time, you don't have to worry about the *ball* hitting you." I knew the rest.

"It's going to hit me."

"No it's not."

"It *is*, Daddy."

"No goddammit it's *not*."

He returned to the stands. "It is," I said. I squared back in, bat held back and high like a good Latin hitter (I was a superbly coached coward), watched the pitcher wind up, and closed my eyes so I could not move away, like a horse with a sack on its head in a barn fire. The ball hit me cleanly in the head with enough force to put me on the very plate, breathing clay.

"You've *killed* him, you son of a bitch!" my mother is alleged to have screamed, hitting my father. I was awarded first base and so became the only Mullet base runner all season, as I recall. I did not score. Years later, on a championship team in Jacksonville (we were the Green Turtles this time, but no scrubs, and we had the supreme pleasure of beating a team that called itself the Jets; if I were to get on a team today, it would be the Manatees or Sea Cucumbers, I'm sure), I was batting over .600 yet was still afraid, at heart, of the ball, and today when I see Dickie Thon hit in the eye in Houston badly enough to speculatively end his career, I feel justified.

The next application of the formula was not *ad hoc* but *in genere*. If I ever got a whipping at school, I was promised a further and worse one at home. This made a pretty good boy of me. In fact, I suspect some early intimation of this public-private double whammy helped little Gary and his aunt in their rout of me, and I have even today a fear of appointed authority that might seem more appropriate in Moscow. I pay unmerited invoices. I contest no parking ticket. I am working now almost fifteen years devising a way of repairing damages for a harmless, prank theft in college. Police make me babble. I volunteer for breathalyzers lest they think ill of me.

The four shots of my father may suggest his power in the application of threatened force. From these images, and probably from my parents' collection of Elvis Presley's early 45's ("Hound Dog," "Heartbreak Hotel," "Don't Be Cruel"—these were their good years; in the sixties they graded into Perry Como and Andy Williams and Ray Coniff and His Singers), which I played relentlessly, I got the impression that there was a closer-than-usual alignment between my father and Elvis. His Marine dress-blues portrait—disappeared, but similar to the cocky portrait here—is alleged to have been mailed home for distribution among the girls waiting for the war to end and the fun to begin, and the running-lizard open-field gridiron cameo was already in the public domain. My conclusion: the old man was fast, insouciant, competent enough to need make no idle threat.

In the ninth grade I sat one day with a girl on a school bus rather than, as rule stipulated, with the boys, for the simple reason that boys were three-to-a-seat and you could sit two-to-a-seat on the less crowded girls' side. Ahead of me another boy sat with another girl. This was not an altogether irregular infraction, but on this particular morning the driver asked us to separate. We did not. We were summoned, the fellow ahead of me and I, to the Dean of Boys' office.

There it was alleged that we had been told by the driver to move, had done so to his satisfaction (the driver was honest in his assumption), and had then had the temerity to move back. "No, sir," I said, digging our grave a bit deeper with my ever-honest teeth. "We never moved."

"You *never moved*," the Dean said.

"No, sir," we both said.

"What if there'd been a fire on the bus and the driver told you to move?"

"That's different," one of us must have essayed. (I recall *fire* being involved in curious relation also to long hair and leaning back in desks during these enlightened years. How anyone survived public education where I took it I do not know.)

We explained that the segregated-sex rule made no sense to us because of the crowding on the male half of the bus, that girls were often sitting alone. Our interrogator, I'll call him MacDavid, here turned in his oak swivel chair and stared out of the window for a full three minutes, leaving us standing in front of his desk. During his study of the outdoors, he sighed heavily and rubbed his stubble. At last he swung around.

"Boys, do you know *why* we have this rule?"

That was precisely it! We couldn't begin to know. "No, sir."

"Well, I'll tell you." More face-rubbing—his beard, at 10:30, was as heavy as card teeth for cleaning files. "This year you know we are *integrated*."

"Yes, sir," one of us must have said, allowing the other to work on this surprising tack.

"Well, how would you feel," the Dean said to Greg (Greg Strontem, whose real name I'll use on pain of suit to correctly honor the small heroism he was about to effect), "how would you feel if one of them *sat with your sister*?"

(I realize this tableau is perhaps incredibly close to the hackneyed *marrying* of one's sister, but you may as well believe this went down as depicted—I could render it less trying to credulity by adjusting some fictional stops.)

(One other thing: it had come out in prior testimony that *I* was sitting with Greg's sister, a fact we naively submitted in the hope that the crime of

sitting with girls would somehow be mitigated by the sister-brother complicity, as though in fact we might have all just been on some kind of cozy, non-
sexual double date.)

To the Dean's question, Greg Strontem said, "I wouldn't mind, if he was a
nice guy."

"I didn't *ask* you what kind of GUY he was! How would you *feel?*" The
Dean of Boys was right worked up. We were oddly calmed by his seething—
relieved to discover, I suppose, a larger issue in all of this than our simple
disobedience.

Calmly, Greg again started: "Well, if he was a nice guy and all—"

"*I don't care what kind of guy he is!*" the Dean shouts.

I am at this point a virtual spectator, in a kind of intellectually and sexually rapt state: *it was me*, I'm thinking, *I'm the guy.* If I were black, what
more harm might I have done? I am horny enough at this age to do sufficient
harm, you may be sure, and perhaps I'm amused at this, but to state I was
lost in complex and moral speculations is not correct. I was taking, simply,
an odd pleasure standing on these junior-high gallows for my imaginary foil,
thinking it would be nice to . . . whatever with Greg's sister, thinking maybe
I wasn't *nearly* so nice as our imaginary black, and enjoying my accidental
subbing for him.

Meanwhile, the Dean is steaming, nostrils burning, when Greg says, "I
wouldn't care."

"You wouldn't care."

"No, sir."

"How about you?" the Dean says to me.

"I wouldn't care. *I* was the one sitting—"

"God *damn!* That's not the point!"

We stood there, waiting for the point. Here it came.

"You can take swats or bus suspension."

I ask how many swats versus how many days off the bus, and the Dean
asks me if there's something *wrong* with me, and I say no, I'd just like to
know (I am calculating the odds also of keeping this whole affair quiet at
home—it will be remembered that the duplicate whipping will presumably
be in effect). It comes out to three swats or three weeks, and that's too long
to ride a bike ten miles, so we get our asses blasted smartly three times
with a polished one-by-two wielded by a state-funded, certified, pensioned
redneck.

I go home and keep all of this a secret, and don't know what might have happened had I revealed it. I suspect the I'll-hit-you double jeopardy or some perverse latter-day expression of it would have obtained, but I like also to think I might have gotten the bastard fired. Of all one's dumb days, of all the stupid things one has said and done and keeps saying and doing, of all one's small retreats from honor, this is one event I would yet like to play differently. I would like to get a hammer and go back and repay the Dean. I wish I had said to him that I'd accept neither punishment until I called the NAACP and both our parents, for starters, and my family's lawyer, and seen what might have happened.

And I do not feel so hot today for the very suspicion that one is yet being told by brutes to sit against the wall while the non-meek inherit the earth, to not sit with the girls for reasons you'd never guess. One gets the large feeling of returning home most days without hitting back. That little nausea is at the root, perhaps, of deciding to write—deciding at last, however feebly, to defend oneself, to hit back.

The Pacific WWII scenes combined in my mind with the running lizard and the Presley sneer to create an image of carefully successful violence on demand, an instantaneous access to violence so successful, upon demand, in fact, that its threat your way would motivate a child to hammer another in the sacral plate, take a beanball with grace, conceal the graceless hazing of juveniles by a grown bigot. It is, though, this violence, an enviable thing to me, a thing which, if I had, I could . . . relax. The connection may be specious, but look (in the Pacific shots) how relaxed these guys are! It looks like a movie set—my father could be Martin Sheen filming *Apocalypse Now* in the Philippines. One sees no photographs of Vietnam that suggest this quality of comfort within war. Yet this was war. Things were nasty enough that my father deliberately tells no war stories other than these: (1) The Japs were tougher than we were, and unjustly provoked into fighting by our limiting their efforts at peaceful expansion (I have always found this a generous sentiment to come from an All-Southern halfback who claims this fighting "walked his legs off"—to an unresilient and unplayable condition upon his return at the seeming prime of twenty-four). And (2) a tale of a typhoon that hit and kept hitting for three days, driving rain so hard it cut flesh, ripping tents which were tied to a cable strung between two earth graders, and even the earth graders were moved! After the blow, they emerge from the shredded canvas heaps, and "Yankees" who have never seen hurricanes, he says, are "white as sheets" for another three days. Then they get

Padgett Powell

back to the business at hand, and though the Japs' *soldiers* might be a little more bulldoggy than ours, our scientists appear a little quicker than theirs, and so a lot more of these relaxed Martin Sheens than might have come home *do* come home, and with these "preternatural tans" (just read this somewhere) claim wives away from the high school boys and put on the ground the next wave of Pacific soldiers and record their childhoods in these snappy little Eastman Kodak works of art. At any rate, though, we struck back.

The remaining pictures sustain or impel one toward the odd resolution to strike back on paper. The first rather obviously: evolving from her very book is my maternal grandmother, whose five novels, one dedicated to me and read at an early age (so early that I wasn't sure I wasn't *in the book*),

and whose estranged life in New York lent hope of one's own eventual writerly bigtime (I have always preferred to believe, though, that the publication party pictured here was not in New York but in Port St. Joe, Florida, where the novel is set).

What you need, when you begin to dabble with the fool notion that you can somehow take a hammer to the world with paper and print, is good, solid convincing that you are nut enough to support the notion long enough to strike. My pistoling, noveling grandmother is here seen posing not with an uncle of mine, as I thought for years, but with her new husband (he is both the gangster and the football player). She has spurned, it would seem, my

real grandfather, seen here (with my mother) gaunt and stern, an accomplished scrubland jack-of-all-trades (house painting to school principaling) whose salient characteristic seems in the long view to have been bad luck with his women (his third wife, no picture, is believed by at least three surviving members of our shrinking clan to have poisoned him—twice). He is unique among us also for his temperate stand against alcohol, one he took after winding up in jail *both* times in his life he drank. The rest of us are openly practicing clinical cases of one description or another.

Here, in fact, balding, is my other grandfather, about whom I know only that he was "a hair-jerker" (my father's phrase, and indicative, one may presume, of the somewhat milder I'll-hit-you disposition), and that he was a Federal beverage agent during Prohibition who successfully used the job to protect Alachua County bootleggers. And my paternal grandmother (of the cross-legged women, she's on the left): in my long, undetailed view, she was an avid poker player who belted jiggers and shuffled cards with the same rapid motions of a person washing his hands.

The Feds for whom my grandfather worked popped in one day with a bit of a plan. They put my grandmother in the back seat, had my grandfather drive, and went to a known bootlegger's where my grandfather was to ask for

whiskey himself—a ploy designed to prove he was in cahoots not merely at the level of graft but, as it were, up to his gills. Presumably the total want of arrests in his county had raised a brow or two.

At the bootlegger's, my grandfather placed the order (of a family friend, to boot), and from the backseat, where she had been put to prevent her phoning ahead, my grandmother called ahead anyway with a "high sign," as family legend puts it—what specifically she did that warned a man outside the car, without signaling those inside the car, I don't know, but I suspect it came from the theater of poker.

Once, forty years later, she escaped from a nursing home as I arrived to visit. The staff was indeed hair-tearing, frantic, for she was frail and it was hot and she was gone. Apparently inserting the family template for escape, I walked directly across the most dangerous thoroughfare adjacent the home, into the absolute densest apartment complex in sight, and then directly to the small entrance foyer where she had given out, pink-gowned and blinking in the sun. "What *took* you so long!" she said to me in a high, dramatic over-drawl that would have been the envy of all the bad actresses who have ever played Blanche Dubois, and she was baffled that I did not, according to our imaginary conspiracy, provide the means necessary to effect her complete getaway.

The pictures of my mother should speak of a theatricality undiluted, and the one of my brothers of white mice, their hair kept short during these Goldwater-all-the-way days for experimental purposes. And here I hold one of the free world's last indigo snakes (I mean, we needed no state permit to possess this now on-the-brink fellow)—drawn to snakes early, I was, because by my lights they truly can find no real way of hitting back, and I am here prepared to defend them with the zeal of a carnival barker.

My conclusion: there is photographic evidence of enough nut blood and thespian gameness in this my clan to get any but the truly uninterested off to a well-grounded start in the art of assembling strange truths into less strange lies—to a soaring faith in the improbable belief that with pen and paper one can hit back.

D I D N ' T   M E A N

G O O D - B Y E

S H E I L A   B O S W O R T H

My mother was the blue-eyed beauty of her family, a family blessed with other, lesser beauties of Irish blood. That was the opinion of many people, including her sister, Justine. Justine was ten years older than Jennie, but she permitted herself none of the customary privileges of older sisters; Justine deferred to Jennie, even, apparently in photographs. There is a picture of the sisters, taken by Justine's husband, Jamie, on the day in 1943 that Jennie announced her engagement to the Navy flier who would become my father. Uncle Jamie was a fine amateur photographer, but this photograph of his seems off-center. The imbalance, I think, is due to the subtle dominance of the lady on the left, my mother; it is the doing not of the photographer but of his subjects.

On a winter Sunday years later, Uncle Jamie took other photographs. (He set his camera on a tripod and affixed a timer to the shutter-release button to get the picture of Justine and himself staring out from armchairs in my parents' parlor.) By then, my father's gold Navy wings were decorating a teddy bear's chest in my baby sister's nursery, and Uncle Jamie had grown sick enough to die before summer came.

Two out of the three children in our family knew my uncle was dying, as well as most of the adults. Uncle Jamie himself was reportedly in the dark; Aunt Justine had told him he was suffering from an acute calcium deficiency. Treece, our cook, gave my sister, Bonnie, and me the facts on Uncle Jamie's condition only a few days after he became ill.

"Last Friday noon, your Uncle Jamie took your Aunt Justine down to the

French Quarter for her birthday dinner," Treece said. "Soon as the desserts gets there, your Uncle Jamie's hand starts to rocking, and it knock his spoon up against his teeth. His ice-cream go all down his front. Then he fell out on the floor. Then your aunt-ee, she get down on all fours and grab hold his tongue—"

"What were they acting like that for?" I said, astonished.

"Because he's got something *wrong* with him, dummy," said Bonnie.

I remember it was Halloween, and we were in the kitchen. My sister and I were dressed alike in multicolored satin gypsy costumes, our faces and lips rouged. We weren't going anyplace, though. We were getting ready to hand out bags of candy to those children whose parents were so ill bred as to allow their offspring to beat on neighbors' doors and yell "Trick-or-Treat."

"What *was* wrong with your uncle going to *stay* wrong with him too," said Treece. She filled a small paper sack with Michigan mints and Red Hots and twisted the bag shut. "Your grandmamma say he ain't going to last out past next Easter. He got him an un-operatable tumor on his brains."

Then it was no longer Halloween, it was a winter afternoon just before Valentine's Day, and my aunt and uncle had come, as they often did, to have Sunday dinner with us. Now it was Aunt Justine who sat behind the steering wheel of the green Studebaker and Uncle Jamie who rode on the passenger's side during the long drive from Whitegrove to New Orleans. Whitegrove, located upriver, in Napoleonville, was a big, ruined-looking house with lino-leum laid over hardwood floors and with mosquito nests in the armoires. It had belonged to Uncle Jamie's family for generations, and had once been the centerpiece of a grand sugar plantation, but now Whitegrove was falling down around itself. "Whitegrove. Jesus Christ," I had heard my father say. "Terrific little hangout, if you happen to be the Prisoner of Zenda." Then he'd grinned at my mother and winked at Bonnie and me.

The Sunday Uncle Jamie took the photographs, my parents were absent from the dinner table. My mother was upstairs in bed; the new baby, Con-stance Ann, lay next to her, in a wicker cradle. My father had been missing since the night before, when he'd left the house with a flask of bourbon and someone he called "Benny the Bum"—Mr. Ben Lofton, who was visiting from Charlotte, North Carolina. Ben Lofton had been my father's closest friend during World War II, had been his co-pilot and then his best man, and had most recently been refused access to our guest room by my mother, on the grounds he was accompanied to New Orleans by a young lady who was not his wife. I was sorry Ben Lofton was not staying in our guest room, because during his previous visit I had fallen in love with him. He was as handsome as a television cowboy and liked to walk about the house in his bare feet.

Without my parents and Ben Lofton at the table to tease one another and laugh among themselves, dinner seemed to last as long as eleven o'clock Mass had. I sat across from Uncle Jamie and watched his hands as they operated his knife and fork and lifted his water goblet to his lips. The hands looked steady enough. They didn't "rock," and Uncle Jamie did not "fall out" on the floor or otherwise surprise me until just before the praline parfaits were served, when he suddenly upset his wine glass while spooning ice-cubes from a cut-glass bowl in the center of the table onto his bread and

My father, Raif, second officer from the right (in light coat); his friend and co-pilot, Ben Lofton (fourth from left). At the races, Washington Park, in Chicago, near Glenview, Illinois, Naval Air Station. November 1943. Photographer unknown.

butter plate. My grandmother moaned and Aunt Justine asked him what he thought he was doing.

"Because I happen to prefer my butter hard, that's what I'm doing," explained Uncle Jamie. His chin quivered as if he might cry. Before Aunt Justine could say any more, Treece was at my uncle's side, mopping up the spill with a damp rag. "That ain't nothing," she said to Uncle Jamie, not looking at him. "You want some more wine?"

"I think not," said my grandmother. Lowering her voice she added to the room at large, "Acts more like a child than Bonnie here."

That was certainly true. Bonnie already knew how to order from the menu at Galatoire's and could find her way, unescorted, from a parlor car to the diner on the Panama Limited.

After dinner, we filed into the parlor. My grandmother sank into a chair near the cold fireplace and Bonnie and I headed for the black marble hearth and looked up the chimney for bats. My father had given Bonnie a picture book featuring bats; bats had become the most recent objects of her affection, and I was determined to find a real one for her. After a few minutes, I handed her, in desperation, a dead moth, hoping halfheartedly that she wouldn't notice the difference.

"Dead moth," said Bonnie, brushing it out of her hand. "Keep looking."

Uncle Jamie was loading his camera and he called to Bonnie and me to move closer to my grandmother so he could take our picture. Aunt Justine interrupted her supervising of the camera-loading, and came over and brushed fireplace ash off Bonnie's dress and mine and led us to my grandmother's chair.

"Bonnie's black velvet, cool as black marble to touch," said Aunt Justine. "That sounds like the first line of a poem, don't you think, Mother?"

"Don't *I* think?" said my grandmother. "Why are you suddenly concerned with what *I* think? If you cared what *I* think, then why would you have become a nurse?"

Aunt Justine had become a nurse twenty years before because her fiancé at the time had told her he wouldn't wait for her to finish medical school. Then the fiancé ran off to Maryland.

"Jamie, now don't go shooting the back of my head," said Aunt Justine. She arranged Bonnie and me for the photograph and retreated to study the effect.

"If she doesn't let go of my dress," announced Bonnie.

I let go of Bonnie's hem and transferred my grasp to my grandmother's silk-covered knee.

"Where are you going, Justine?" called Uncle Jamie. "Come get in this one!"

"Next one," said Aunt Justine. "I have to go out to the kitchen a minute. I forgot to tell Treece which portion of the rib roast she can take home."

"Now *why*?" said my grandmother, shaking her head, after Justine had gone. "Oh well, it can't be helped. I've never met a Negro in his right mind who could stand Justine, anyway."

Bonnie and my grandmother and I sat in silence for a few minutes and watched Uncle Jamie glide forward and back, forward and back, while he stared into the top of his camera.

"Guess what Treece just said to me," said Aunt Justine, reappearing.

"No telling," sighed my grandmother.

"She don't take orders from nobody but Mr. Raif and Miss Jennie."

From the kitchen came the sound of a metal utensil being ground up in the disposer.

"Another piece of your sister's flat silver gone," said my grandmother, when the clattering ceased. "And if she woke up Jennie and the baby with that racket, you know who's responsible!"

Uncle Jamie looked up uncertainly from his camera, as if he were afraid my grandmother meant him.

"Jamie, honey, for God's sake, will you stop shuffling up and down and just take the picture?" said Aunt Justine. She looked at my grandmother. "She's sulking, of course. Him and his friend not showing up, after she went to all the trouble of Greenbeans Alciatoire and two yam pies."

"I couldn't be less interested," said my grandmother, arching her eyebrows and glancing at Bonnie and me.

"Smile, sugar," called Uncle Jamie, and Bonnie ducked her head and deepened her dimples, although I was sure he'd been talking to me. I was Uncle Jamie's godchild, his favorite, the only one in the world he would still allow to touch his hair. I heard the camera click before I had time to smile.

My grandmother, my sister Bonnie (center), and I, at my parents' house in New Orleans. Photo by Uncle Jamie.

Suddenly Uncle Jamie placed his camera on a three-legged stand and rushed towards us, calling to Aunt Justine to go sit in an armchair, flapping his arms at Bonnie and my grandmother and me, the way I'd seen him shoo away pigeons in Audubon Park. Watching him, I wondered if the thing on his brain made his head hurt. Then I thought about asking him to take me to the carousel at that park again. If his head hurt, he wouldn't have to chase pigeons for me. He could sit on a bench near the Flying Horses and watch me as I came around.

I heard the camera click again while Aunt Justine and Uncle Jamie sat staring at it as if they were waiting for it to say something to them.

"Who wants to watch the invisible genie take one more photograph?" called Uncle Jamie from his chair.

"I wouldn't mind watching him," I said.

"Invisible means you can't watch it," Bonnie pointed out.

"Exactly, darling," said my grandmother. "Now. Who wants to watch me go upstairs and lie down before my head snaps off my neck?"

Aunt Justine and Uncle Jamie at my parents' house in New Orleans. Photo taken by Uncle Jamie's camera set on a tripod with timer affixed to shutter-release button.

"I might go up and lie down awhile, too," said Aunt Justine. "One of the guest rooms."

"As long as you don't come out reeking of Jennie's perfumes," said my grandmother. "You're not the one who's still listening night and day to how you sailed into her hospital room, drenched in her best Chanel, the night Raif took you to Antoine's."

"He could hardly have taken *her* to Antoine's, could he?" said Aunt Justine, getting up from her chair. Her voice sounded high and frail, like Treece's voice when she sang the blues. "She was flat on her back in Hôtel Dieu, recuperating from a Caesarean section performed at the patient's request! And I, I was dead on my feet from sleeping there on a horrible cot with her—for how many nights? Until my own sick husband—"

But my grandmother had left the room and started up the stairs. I saw her shadow pause for a moment in the sunlight on the landing, then move on. I heard the slow sound of her footsteps along the upstairs hall.

Aunt Justine walked to the doorway and stood looking out at the stairway, her back to the three of us in the parlor. She lifted her pretty hands to her hair and loosened one of the hairpins in her auburn braid, then another.

"I wonder," she said, after a while, not turning around, "I wonder can I leave Jamie alone down here with the girls?"

My aunt often spoke aloud to herself, and when she did I usually had trouble understanding what she meant. Maybe Aunt Justine was afraid Uncle Jamie would get sick and Bonnie and I wouldn't be able to help him. Then I thought about what I'd heard my father tell my mother a while ago. "Jamie might just as soon strangle Justine as look at her, the state his brain is in." Bonnie had heard it, too. Maybe Bonnie should tell Aunt Justine she was the one who ought to be afraid of Uncle Jamie, not us.

Uncle Jamie was staring at his shoes and frowning, as if he were trying to remember something. Maybe he was trying to remember some magic word that would make Justine leave him downstairs with Bonnie and me. Then Bonnie said, "I'm not afraid! Besides Treece is right out there in the kitchen." She slipped her hand into Uncle Jamie's and he looked up from staring at his shoes and smiled at her.

Aunt Justine had finished loosening her braid and when she finally turned to look at us her hair was hanging to her waist. Her hair was rippled and spoilt from always being tightly braided. "Afraid? What's there to be afraid of?" she said. "That's the silliest thing I ever heard. Who have you children been listening to?"

Sheila Bosworth

Bonnie shrugged. Her hand still in Uncle Jamie's, she led him over to the bookcase, where her basket of valentines lay on a low shelf. She began telling Uncle Jamie that she had learned how to spell "love," and how to print her name.

When I looked back at Aunt Justine, she was standing so still that I wanted to make her laugh, the way Uncle Jamie and Bonnie were laughing over the valentines. I ran over to her, placed a strand of her hair under my nose like a mustache and worked my eyebrows up and down. Bonnie had made the same face, using a comb for the mustache, after we'd seen Groucho Marx on television one night.

Apparently, Aunt Justine had never seen Groucho Marx. Drawing back a little, she pried my fingers from around her hair and said, "Little ladies don't wipe their noses on people's hair. Run on, now, and show your uncle your *own* valentines."

"I don't have any valentines. I don't go to school yet," I began, but Aunt Justine was already halfway up the stairs.

"This one's for Marie Spenlou," Bonnie said to Uncle Jamie. "Marie Spenlou is the one who has the crippled cat, remember? I told you about the cat already."

Uncle Jamie sat crosslegged on the floor, his back against the bookcase, examining Marie Spenlou's valentine. Then he looked up at me. "Let's see *your* valentines, sugar."

"I don't have any," I said. "I don't go to school yet."

"You do, too," said Bonnie.

"Where do you go?" said Uncle Jamie.

"I don't go anywhere," I said. "I stay here. With Treece."

"You do, too, have a *valentine*," said Bonnie. "You know. The one you picked out for Treece." She turned to Uncle Jamie. "She has a valentine *present*. She wrapped it up. She's going to give it to Treece for a surprise."

While Uncle Jamie and Bonnie looked at the next valentine in the basket, I got Treece's present out of the piano bench. It was *Black Beauty*, a book with a shiny orange cover and a picture of the horse's face on the front, staring out from its stall. Bonnie and I had begun wrapping it days ago, using pack after pack of white tissue paper we'd found in my mother's sewing room. The trouble was, no matter how much paper we used, Black Beauty's face still showed through. Treece wouldn't be surprised at all, she would know the minute I handed it to her what her present was. The package had grown so thick and misshapen with paper that I had trouble holding it, but I managed to hand it to Uncle Jamie.

"What's this?" I asked him.

"*Black Beauty*," said Uncle Jamie. "There's his face, right there on the front."

"See?" I said to Bonnie.

"Put some more paper on it," said Bonnie.

"I don't have any more paper. I'm tired of wrapping up *Black Beauty*. I want to do something fun. I want to play a game."

"What do you want to play, sugar?" said Uncle Jamie.

"Restaurant," I said. "Let's play restaurant."

"Uh-uh," said Bonnie. "Treece."

"She's gone," I said. "I heard Buster Leggins come to the back door and get her."

Buster Leggins was Treece's husband. He was also, according to my father, something called a "roughneck" on a kind of boat called an oil rig. The only other roughneck I knew of was a little girl with a skinny head and no underpants who'd been called "roughneck" by my grandmother the day she'd pushed Bonnie off a merry-go-'round at City Park. Every time I thought of Buster Leggins, I pictured him pushing people off an oil rig.

"How do you play restaurant?" said Uncle Jamie, getting slowly to his feet. He held on to the bookcase a minute after he was standing.

"First we get to wear Treece's aprons," explained Bonnie. "Then we set the table in the kitchen and the table in the dining room. We get to use the pretty dishes and the silver forks and all the best glasses. Then we put water in all the pots on the stove and pretend like we're cooking it."

"We pour water in the glasses on the tables, too," I said.

"Then somebody's the waiter and somebody's the customer and somebody's the cook. We can take turns being the customer because nobody wants to be him," continued Bonnie.

"I'll be the customer," offered Uncle Jamie. "You just tell me what you want me to do."

"Well, see, we don't really know what to do, because we've never really played this before because Treece won't let us," said Bonnie over her shoulder, leading the way to the kitchen. "And we can't reach the stuff, the good glasses and stuff, by ourselves."

"You just tell me what to do," repeated Uncle Jamie.

The sun was going down. In the kitchen only a bluish electric light shone above the stove, and somehow it felt colder in the kitchen than it did in the rest of the house.

"Turn on a light," Bonnie said to Uncle Jamie. In the dimness we heard glass breaking, and then the overhead light flickered on and we saw several jagged pieces of varicolored porcelain on the brick floor near Uncle Jamie's feet.

"What's that?" said Uncle Jamie. "What'd I knock over?"

"It's 'Benny the Bum'," said Bonnie. She stooped and picked up a section of broken porcelain for Uncle Jamie to see.

"'Benny the Bum'?" said Uncle Jamie. "Isn't Benny the Bum your daddy's friend from North Carolina?"

Bonnie was down on the floor, trying to fit together the bigger of the fragments. "This is Benny the Bum, too. See? A figurine. Ben Lofton gave it to Daddy during the war. When Daddy goes out with Ben Lofton, he calls it going bummin'." The three of us looked at what was left of Benny the Bum. It had recently been a hobo leaning against a street light, holding a glass in one hand.

"What's it doing in the kitchen?" I said. "Daddy keeps it on his desk."

"Put the pieces down before you cut yourself, sugar," said Uncle Jamie to Bonnie. "That's right. Just step around them."

"Uncle Jamie, can you lift me up on top of this counter?" I said. "So I can show you which glasses I want you to get down?"

Viewed from higher up, the kitchen looked tilted, and I was suddenly conscious of the slippery soles of my patent leather shoes.

"Uh-oh, I got my dress all wet," said Bonnie, far below, where she was filling a red bean pot with hot water at the sink.

"You forgot Treece's apron," I pointed out. Talking made me dizzier and I tightened my grip on the cabinet next to me. A drop or two of urine rolled down one leg and onto my sock.

Uncle Jamie was transferring the pot of water from the sink to the stove while Bonnie put the silver knives and forks on the table.

"Get the glasses down off that shelf behind you," Bonnie called, glancing up at me.

"Uncle Jamie, you come get them down," I said, but Uncle Jamie was standing on a stool at the other end of the room, sliding the soup tureen from the top of the china cabinet.

"Well if you're too scared to get the glasses!" said Bonnie, staring at me. Using the china drawer pulls below the counter as a sort of step ladder, she reached the top and hoisted herself up to where I stood. Suddenly her face changed and she grabbed my hand, knocking me partway onto the stove top. I felt the unexpected heat from a pilot light beneath my shoe.

"Uncle Jamie, the water's running!" Bonnie cried. "I forgot to turn off the water in the sink."

Uncle Jamie turned to look at us from his perch on top of the stool, still holding the soup tureen in both hands. More dizziness floated over me and I stepped back so I could feel the wall. I felt something hard against my back and then a wild metallic gagging filled the room.

"The disposer, the disposer!" shrieked Bonnie. "Somebody turned on the disposer! Uncle Jamie! Come get me down!"

Then I heard a sound more frightening than the one the disposer was making.

"What the shit going on in this house," said Treece. She was standing at the back door, dressed in her white church dress; behind her loomed Buster Leggins in his Sunday suit and a wide-brimmed straw hat with its crown smashed in on one side.

"Y'all all gonna done fallen!" shouted Treece, bearing down on the counter top where Bonnie and I stood. She reached behind me and switched off the disposer and then swung both of us down, stopping briefly to disengage my foot from a black iron stove burner.

"She wet her pants," announced Bonnie, pointing at me, as soon as her feet touched the ground.

"She ain't the only one, neither," said Buster Leggins. Everybody looked at Uncle Jamie. Buster had maneuvered him into a sitting position on the stool. A dark wetness showed on one side of his trousers, but Uncle Jamie folded his hands on his lap and stared straight ahead, as dignified as if he were listening to a priest give a Sunday sermon.

"And all this ain't the worst of it," said Treece to Buster. "Guess who in the library? Mr. Raif and Mr. Ben Lofton, with Mr. Lofton lady friend. I seen 'em through the window when we come up the drive."

Buster Leggins looked from Treece to Bonnie.

"Where your aunt-ee at?" he asked her.

"I ain't studyin' 'bout dragging the aunt-ee in all this mess," warned Treece, shutting off the water at the sink.

The door to the butler's pantry swung toward us and Ben Lofton came into the kitchen. The collar of his stiff white shirt was unbuttoned and his necktie was pulled to one side. He smelled of whiskey and tobacco, and looking down, I saw that he was barefoot. Love ran through my limbs like wildfire and I longed for a dry dress.

"What y'all doin' out here?" inquired Ben Lofton amiably. "Y'all conducting Sunday school?" He walked over to the refrigerator, weaving slightly, opened the door, and leaned in, his hands on the knees of his pants. "Treece? Where you hiding the Co-Cola and cheese?"

"Mr. Ben, now you ain't had your supper yet," said Treece. "I just stopped back to pick up my section of the rib roast, but I'd be glad to put a yam pie in the oven for you and Mr. Raif and slice you some cold cuts. Go on out to the dining room, why don't you?"

"Buster, what's the happiest day of your life?" said Ben Lofton, his head in the refrigerator.

"In *my* life?" said Buster Leggins. He thought for a minute. "I has to say, the night my kids was born."

"You hear that, Treece?" said Ben Lofton, backing out of the refrigerator with a crock of cheese in one hand. "Didn't you reckon he'd say, the night he married you? Unless that's what he did say, unless you two got married the same night your kids got born. Hell, maybe y'all never got married at all!"

"We married, all right," said Treece, staring darkly at Buster. Treece frequently stared darkly at Buster, for reasons that were unclear to me.

Ben Lofton put the cheese crock on the table and headed towards the pantry. "You ain't making this cheese and cracker hunt any too goddamn easy," he said to Treece. "Where you keep the crackers?"

"I'll get 'em," said Treece.

"So, Buster. You say the happiest day of my life's going to be the day my kid gets born," said Ben Lofton. He looked over at Uncle Jamie on the stool, as if he hadn't noticed him before. "Hey, Jamie! What about you? Were you the happiest the day your kids came?"

Uncle Jamie appeared surprised to have been asked. "I don't have any children," he said. Then he added, "I'm married, all right, though. That's not the main reason I don't have any."

Ben Lofton laughed and clapped a hand onto one of Uncle Jamie's thin shoulders. "You all right, boy," he said. "You a hoot. How come Raif don't ask you down to the Quarter with us? You want to ride back down to the Quarter with Raif and Dottie and me later on this evenin'? You up for that?"

Before Uncle Jamie could answer Ben Lofton, the door to the butler's pantry swung open again and the shiniest lady I'd ever seen came in. Everything on her had a silvery sheen to it, her blond hair, her bright pink lips, her candy-striped dress that bunched over her hips and parted at the back to show her legs above the knees. On her feet she wore high-heeled silver shoes with thin straps around her ankles.

"Dottie!" yelled Ben Lofton. "Come give your Uncle Ben a hug around the neck! Hug Jamie here, too! We fixing to eat Co-Cola and cheese out here! Right, Jamie?"

"I tole you coffee," said Dottie. "You and Raif oughta take some coffee." She had a voice like my grandmother's favorite movie star, Kirk Douglas. She had a dimple in her chin like his, too.

"Dottie, what's the happiest day of your life?"

"You axed me that one time already," said Dottie. She turned to Uncle Jamie. "This joker here keeps axin' everybody that, so they'll ax him the same thing back! Then you know what he says? When they ax him that back, he says, 'The day I waltz down the aisle with Elizabeth Ann on my arm, that's when!'"

"Elizabeth Ann?" echoed Uncle Jamie politely.

"Elizabeth Ann! Elizabeth Ann!" shrieked Dottie. "The goddamn governor's kid! He's marryin' the daughter of the goddamn governor of North Carolina!" A terrible sound, something between a sob and a moo, tore from her throat.

Ben Lofton didn't say anything; he was waving at Aunt Justine, who was suddenly standing in the doorway to the butler's pantry. Or maybe he was waving to my father, who was standing just behind Justine, his hands signaling what looked to me like "Let's go" to Ben Lofton. Aunt Justine's hair was neatly braided across her head again, and her brown dress was as unwrinkled as if it were still on a hanger. She was looking at Dottie, her mouth hanging open.

"Hey there," said Dottie to Aunt Justine. Suddenly she crouched down next to me and grabbed me around the waist. She smelled like the little bottles of ingredients in the perfume-making kit my father had bought Bonnie and me at F. A. O. Schwarz. "Is this your little girl? She's adorable!"

"She's my niece," said Aunt Justine. "I haven't any children."

Dottie let go of me and stood up, swaying a little on the silver heels. "Me, neither," she said. "My ex-husband couldn't thrill me."

Aunt Justine made a strange sound in her throat and my father began signaling "Let's go" to Ben Lofton again.

Ben Lofton said, "Raif, you and Jamie here and Dottie and me, we're all going down to the Quarter! Come on, everybody, let's go. I had enough cheese and crackers. Never *could* find the Co-Cola."

"Jamie isn't going any place," said Aunt Justine. "My husband is ill, in case you're blind, deaf, and dumb, Ben Lofton. And Raif, Jennie's awake and asking for you upstairs."

"She is!" said Ben. "Well hell, I didn't know Jennie was up to seeing everybody! Let's all go up to Jennie's room and ask her what the happiest day of her life was." He looked at Aunt Justine. "I bet you'd guess the happiest day of Raif's life was when he married your pretty sister, wouldn't you? Well it wasn't though! Tell her, Raif."

"I forgot," said my father.

"The day he got his wings! His gold goddamn Navy wings! That's what ol' Raif said!"

All the men in the room, with the exception of Buster Leggins, started laughing. Then Ben Lofton stepped on a piece of Benny the Bum and started bleeding. Blood from his bare foot ran across the brick floor of the kitchen.

"Well hell," said Ben Lofton, sounding puzzled. He lifted one foot and watched the blood run out of it onto the bricks. "What the hell is this?"

"Benny the Bum," said Bonnie, holding up a jagged piece of porcelain.

"Which of you girls broke your father's porcelain figurine?" said Aunt Justine. "Your father treasured that figurine! It was a memento of his Navy days!"

"Yeah, shame on whoever done it," drawled Buster Leggins. "That there doll better than the Extinguish Flyin' *Cross*."

Aunt Justine turned and looked at Buster. Her face was very white. "You take off your hat when you're in this house, you goddamn nigger," she said. She hadn't even raised her voice.

Buster Leggins looked steadily back at her. "Yes ma'am, Miss Justine. Look like it had slip my remembrance for a minute, about the hat." His big hands lay very still at his sides.

"Jesus Christ, Justine, you're a nurse," said my father. "Can't you fix his foot?"

"Oh a nurse," said Dottie to Aunt Justine. "Well la de da, I knew we had something in common, dearie. My pop's a barber."

I was looking at Uncle Jamie when it happened, because I heard the metal legs of the stool where he was sitting begin to rock on the brick floor, and I turned in the direction of the sound.

Uncle Jamie's hands began to shake, and he lifted them to his mouth, exposing the wet mark on his trousers. His eyes moved quickly back and forth, stopped, then rolled back in his head, the whites showing. His tongue hung from one side of his mouth and he made a choking sound.

"Oh my God," whispered Dottie.

"Hold on! Hold on, now!" cried Buster Leggins. He caught Uncle Jamie while he was midway to the floor and falling sideways, just before the stool clanged onto the bricks. Uncle Jamie writhed and jerked in Buster's arms, his face darkening, a rattling sound coming from his throat. He looked to me like a man being tickled by someone I couldn't see, by the invisible genie, perhaps, tickled till he couldn't breathe.

"Put him on the sofa in the playroom," said Aunt Justine. "If you can just get him on the sofa, I know what to do."

The sofa in the playroom, a bright yellow sofa. There it is, in the background of a photograph my father took of my sisters, my aunt, my grandmother, and me the Christmas after Uncle Jamie died. I thought I had forgotten the color of that sofa, the events of that afternoon, until, years later,

From right: *My grandmother, my sister Constance Anne (on my grandmother's lap), my sister Bonnie, Aunt Justine, and I (looking at camera). Photograph taken by my father, Raif, the Christmas after Uncle Jamie died, at my parents' house in New Orleans.*

I began to suffer from a recurrent nightmare. In the dream I was dressed in yellow, a color I have seldom worn, and I was suffocating, something wound tighter and tighter around my chest, my neck, until the illusion of being unable to breathe awakened me. Finally I told a doctor about the dream. "Can you remember being overstimulated in some way as a child? Touched, or tickled perhaps," the doctor said. "And why yellow? What comes to mind?"

And then one day, as I looked through a box of old photographs, Uncle Jamie came to mind. Uncle Jamie on a bright yellow sofa, struggling as if he couldn't breathe; Aunt Justine, half on top of him, pressing something against his tongue, holding his head, the folds of her dress crushed beneath Uncle Jamie's legs.

"You realize you can't bring him here anymore, don't you?" said my mother, the evening of the day it happened. "It's—it wouldn't be fair to anyone, to him, to us, to the children. And my nerves, and the new baby . . . you know what I mean, don't you, Justine?"

"Know what I mean," repeated Uncle Jamie. He lay quietly on the sofa now, but still I was afraid to take his hand. So I sat nearby, on the rug, until they left for Whitegrove, for home. "Know what I mean," he said, and tried to wink at me. And I suppose I did know, in some measure, even then. I wished I didn't, though. I wished I didn't know what Uncle Jamie meant. I wished Uncle Jamie didn't mean good-bye.

REACHING

THE STARS

MY LIFE AS A

FIFTIES GROUPIE

BOBBIE ANN MASON

*I*n the late nineteen-fifties, when I was a teenager, I held a national office, published a journal, was interviewed on television and radio, and traveled widely to places like Cincinnati and Detroit and Blytheville, Arkansas. I was a shy, backward, anti-social country kid living on a farm near Mayfield, Kentucky, a hundred and fifty miles from the nearest city, Nashville, but I was ambitious and determined to hit the big time—or at least meet somebody famous. The first star I met was Gene Autry's dumpy sidekick in the floppy hat, Smiley Burnette. I was about thirteen when he came to town for a show at the Princess Theatre. You could buy a picture of him for a dollar or pay a dollar to have your picture taken with him. Smiley hooked his arm around my shoulders and posed me for the camera, but when I asked him to sign my autograph book he snarled, "I don't autograph nothing but the pictures for sale."

The second star on my life list was Tony Martin, the crooner who sang "There's No Tomorrow" and was married to Cyd Charisse. He came to town to publicize Tony Martin suits, which were manufactured by the Merit Clothing Company, the local factory where my mother worked. She and I went to

I was about thirteen when Smiley Burnette came to town.

the Hall Hotel and gawked at him as he got off the elevator. He was surprisingly short.

But from the time I was a child singers impressed me more than movie stars did. I listened to the radio constantly. Perry Como and Patti Page dominated the daytime airwaves in those days, but late on Saturday nights the radio blared out strange music: "John R here, way down South in Dixie, 1510 on the dial, fifty thousand watts of joy! WLAC, Nashville, Tennessee."

John R played raunchy, stomping-and-shouting blues numbers by black singers like Big Bill Broonzy and Memphis Slim and Little Junior Parker, Little Walter, T-Bone Walker, Elmore James, and Big Joe Turner. The theme song on John R's show was "Dig These Blues," a slow, rolling piano blues. John R was white, but he sounded black. WLAC advertised mysterious products—Silky Strate, White Rose petroleum jelly, "lifetime" Bibles, and soul medallions. My parents and I stayed up late and turned the radio up loud, staring in amazement at our huge console, as big as a jukebox, as it blared out wild music. John R and another white disk jockey, Gene Nobles, who had a show earlier in the evening, played what they called "droopy-drawers songs" (the slow stuff) and "mean, low-down songs." The mean ones sounded dangerous. I could feel the power of big men stomping into their houses and dragging out their women when they'd been untrue. In the droopy-drawers songs, they cried their hearts out. John R talked through the songs: "Have mercy, baby! . . . Come on, honey. . . . Man, don't that tear you up?" Ruth Brown's "Mama, He Treats Your Daughter Mean" tore me up bad.

Gene Nobles also played some bland white imitations of these risqué rhythm-and-blues songs—especially "cover" versions from Dot Records, owned by his sponsor, Randy's Record Shop in Gallatin, Tennessee. Randy's artists included Pat Boone and the Fontane Sisters. His star group was the Hilltoppers.

The Hilltoppers, I decided, represented everything I had ever felt and dreamed about my life. As I picked blackberries or hoed vegetables in the scorching morning sun, I longed to travel and see the world. The turbulent music on WLAC expressed my frustration, and the Hilltoppers made me feel there was an answer—some release from the cycle of the seasons, the planting and harvesting. (I didn't see the glamour in farm life then.) The Hilltoppers' style wasn't exactly Big Bill Broonzy and it wasn't rock and roll yet either—it was sort of like what would happen if Perry Como got hold of some Big Bill Broonzy material—but it grabbed me and shook me up like a religious vision, a calling. This was mainly because the group was from Ken-

Bobbie Ann Mason

The first Hilltoppers group that I met, in Cincinnati. I was fifteen.

THE HILLTOPPERS
FEATURING
JIMMY SACCA

Recording Exclusively
on
DOT RECORDS

tucky. The Hilltoppers were students at Western Kentucky State College, in Bowling Green, where the sports teams were called the Hilltoppers. A Kentucky singing quartet had achieved national fame! The only famous person from Kentucky I had ever heard of besides Abraham Lincoln was Arthur Lake, who played Dagwood in the Blondie-and-Dagwood movies.

The Hilltoppers' first hit was "Trying," a ballad written by one of the original members of the group, Billy Vaughn, and later on they were awarded a gold record for an old Johnny Mercer song, "P.S. I Love You." With the arrival of rock and roll, they started recording livelier imitations of black tunes—"The Door Is Still Open," "Only You," and Ruth Brown's "Teardrops from My Eyes." On some of the songs you could hear a rock-and-roll saxophone or a boogie piano, and even a bass vocal "bum-bum-bum" against the "do-do-do-do-do-do-do" background harmony. But their style was born in an earlier time. Jimmy Sacca, the lead singer, had a strong, distinctive baritone that strained to be a tenor—a cross between matinée-idol crooning and big-band swing. He was a dreamboat.

I started a Hilltoppers fan club, and the day that the package of membership cards, autographed glossy eight-by-ten photographs, and buttons ("I AM A HILLTOPPERS FAN") arrived was the turning point of my life. I advertised for members in Betty Burr's fan-club column in a New York fan magazine,

and for a time my whole life revolved around the mailbox and the radio. I corresponded with a Hilltoppers fan on Long Island who monitored all of New York's radio stations, flipping the dial ceaselessly after school. She constructed elaborate charts, on graph paper, of Hilltoppers airplay. Over the next year, I diligently worked my way up through the Hilltoppers' power structure, mostly by pestering the Hilltoppers' secretary in Gallatin and trying to impress her and the Hilltoppers with my devotion so I could get to meet them, and at last became National President of the Hilltoppers Fan Clubs. As National President, I wrote and mailed a newsletter to three hundred fan-club chapters on an addressographed list—mostly addresses in the exotic environs of New York City. One of my jobs as National President was to conduct request campaigns to DJs. I wrote to DJs in all the big cities:

MEMO FROM THE NATIONAL HILLTOPPERS FAN CLUB
TO: ED BONNER, KXOK, ST. LOUIS
Please play "Do the Bop," the new Hilltoppers record, on your show. It's a big hit! Thank you very much.
—"Till Then,"
BOBBIE MASON, National President

("Till Then" was one of the Hilltoppers' early recordings.)

I prayed for their records to be hits. After reading Norman Vincent Peale, I applied the power of positive thinking to a tune called "Searching," so that the Hilltoppers might earn another gold record.

My memories of the Hilltoppers are vague. I actually got to know them very well, and if they walked into my house today they would be thoroughly familiar to me. I'm sure Jimmy Sacca would give me one of his big bear hugs and we would fall easily into joking conversation. We were friends. But even though I spent a lot of time with the Hilltoppers during my high school years I knew very little about them. I didn't ask about their backgrounds—their parents, brothers and sisters, schooling, and the rest. Background had no meaning to me, because I hadn't been anywhere; where I was going was what counted. The Hilltoppers were stars, brilliant presences, and my function was to promote their fame, so that their glow would rub off on me, like the luminescent stuff from lightning bugs.

In *Hilltoppers Highlights*, the fan-club journal that I wrote and published, I reported what I knew of the Hilltoppers:

"Jimmy Sacca stands six-two and has black hair and brown eyes, loves steak, pizza, spaghetti (you can tell he's Italian!), and when time permits this ex-football player's hobby is miniature golf. He is also accomplished on the clarinet and saxophone. Jimmy comes from Lockport, N.Y.

"Blond, pug-nosed Don McGuire, the ladies' man of the Hilltoppers, surprises everybody with his deep bass voice. He went to Western Ky. on a basketball scholarship and became one of their star players. He planned to

St. Louis, 1956, Jimmy and I.

Jimmy and I with Ed Bonner, KXOK, St. Louis. Ed was my favorite DJ.

be a dentist until stardom beckoned. He hails from Hazard, Ky., is five-eleven, collects sports clothes, plays piano and drums.

"The clown of the Toppers, Seymour ('Sy') Spiegelman of Seneca Falls, N.Y., was Jimmy's roommate at college. He is five-eight, weighs 178, and has black hair and brown eyes. His hobbies are drawing and fishing, and he loves football, swimming and tennis.

"Eddie Crowe, a friend of Jimmy's from Lockport, replaces Billy Vaughn, the original member of the group who penned their first hit, 'Trying'. Eddie lettered in four sports in high school. He's single, girls! In the Hilltoppers' show, he plays the trumpet and does comic impressions—James Cagney, James Stewart, Robert Mitchum."

In time, my mother and I traveled to Cincinnati to see the Hilltoppers perform. It was my first trip anywhere. The ride took sixteen hours, overnight, on a bus that jolted miserably around the curves along the Ohio River. I remember waking up at each stop and checking the town on the map, so I could say I had been there. I was so excited I couldn't eat, even though the group performing was not entirely the original Hilltoppers. While Don and Sy were in the Army (they'd been drafted, and this was just after the Korean War), Jimmy hired a series of replacements. The Hilltoppers were appearing with Barney Rapp's orchestra at the Castle Farms Ballroom in Cincinnati. It was a huge suburban dance hall that was packed with glamorous couples who drank liquor. Women smuggled in whiskey bottles under their wraps: I saw them do it. The Hilltoppers bounded onstage, wearing their red sweaters and beanies with "W" on them—the football sweaters and freshman beanies from their college. (I had ordered a beanie for myself from Western and had considered wearing it that evening, but it didn't go with my taffeta dress and borrowed rhinestone jewelry.) Their act was sensational. They sang all their hits, including "P.S. I Love You," "From the Vine Came the Grape," "I'd Rather Die Young," and my favorite, "Poor Butterfly." Their sound was principally Jimmy Sacca's lead backed up with a simple "doo-wah" harmony. In their sweaters and baggy gray flannels, they swayed from side to side in unison, sort of like cheerleaders. I learned later that their moves had been choreographed. At intermission, I was allowed to go backstage to meet my idols, and during their second show they introduced me proudly to the audience. In the second show, they wore tuxedos.

After the show, they bought my mother and me Cokes and potato chips. The Hilltoppers didn't drink, but they smoked and drove a Cadillac. They

drove us back to the hotel in their sky-blue 1954 Fleetwood, and Jimmy Sacca gave me forty dollars to help operate the fan club.

At school, the Hilltoppers were my secret. I had few friends, because I lived out in the country, and also because I was shy and not interested in suntans and pajama parties. I read a lot: *The Search for Bridey Murphy*, *The Practical Way to a Better Memory*, *The Report on Unidentified Flying Objects*.

The next time we saw the Hilltoppers was in Vincennes, Indiana. Mama and I were walking down the main street from Woolworth's to our hotel there when we spotted the Cadillac. It was the Hilltoppers, arriving in town for their show. I waved at them, and the Cadillac pulled over. Jimmy was driving.

"It's us again!" Mama cried.

Jimmy hopped out and hugged us. While the other members of the group —more replacements—checked into the hotel, Jimmy took us to eat at a grill down the street. We sat in a booth and ordered pork chops with applesauce and French fries.

"Well, what did you think when you heard the news?" Jimmy asked us worriedly.

"I was shocked," I said lamely. I didn't know what to say. I had seen the newspaper: one of the various substitute Hilltoppers had been arrested for possession of marijuana. My mother and I had never heard of marijuana, so the news didn't really faze us.

"I was at the racetrack," Jimmy said. "And the P.A. system called my name. I had no idea he was using the stuff. I fired him so fast he didn't know what hit him."

"He wasn't one of the real Hilltoppers," I said loyally. I longed for the day when Sy and Don would rejoin the group. I knew I would like them, because they looked like such cutups in their pictures. Jimmy and Don and Seymour and Billy, the original group, were all family men, with wives and children.

After we finished eating, Jimmy lit up a Pall Mall, and Mama said, "If y'all come to Mayfield, I'll get you some free Tony Martin suits from the Merit."

"How will you do that?" I asked, surprised.

"Willie Foster will let me have them," Mama said confidently.

Willie Foster was the president of the Merit Clothing Company. We had been to his farm for the annual employees' picnic—fried chicken and roasting ears and washtubs of cold drinks. His farm was like a plantation—a

Carbondale, Illinois: my first meeting with Don, who was just out of the Army and about to rejoin the group.

The first time I met Sy Spiegelman was somewhere in Indiana.

magnificent place with acres of pasture and horses and a little lake with rowboats.

"We'd love to come to Mayfield," Jimmy said. "But you don't have to get us any suits."

"Well, you come, and I'll cook you up a big supper and get you some suits," Mama said. "I used to sew labels in coats, but the foreman told me to slow down because I was making more than the men. So I quit. I could make a dollar an hour, I was so fast." She laughed. "But with all the farm work I didn't have time to sew labels anyway."

"Well, since you quit, they won't let you have any free suits," I argued.

"Oh, Willie wasn't mad at me," Mama said. "Willie's good to his workers. And if the Hilltoppers wore his suits, that would be good publicity."

"Well, gee, Mrs. Mason," Jimmy said. "That would be swell."

He bought us strawberry sundaes and then we went to the show.

After that, Mama and I traveled many places to see the Hilltoppers. We went to Centralia, Illinois; Princeton, Indiana; Herrin, Illinois; Blytheville,

Jimmy and I in Herrin, Illinois, at a ballroom where the Hilltoppers performed. I was fifteen.

Arkansas; and Cape Girardeau, Missouri, as well as St. Louis and Detroit. Daddy had to milk the cows and couldn't go. The Hilltoppers always welcomed us. Don and Sy got out of the Army and took their rightful places in the group. They were boyish, modest, and funny. I adored them. Being a groupie in the fifties was as innocent as the Girl Scouts. The Hilltoppers never even swore around me, except once—the day Jimmy forgot the words to "My Cabin of Dreams," which they lip-synced on Johnny Slagle's "Dance Matinée" on WXYZ in Detroit. They took a protective attitude toward me, and they were crazy about my mother, who didn't put on any airs just because she knew some stars. "I think it's nice they've got that Cadillac and ain't stuckup," Mama said. She still talked about those Tony Martin suits and how good the Hilltoppers would look in them.

My mother and my sister Janice with Jimmy Sacca.

Bobbie Ann Mason

I went to visit Pat Boone Fan Club president Vicki Woodall when Pat Boone appeared in Memphis. This photo was published in 16 Magazine.

During my years with the Hilltoppers, I met lots of stars: Buddy Morrow, Bill Haley and the Comets, Billy Ward and the Dominoes, the Fontane Sisters, the Four Lads, Ted Weems, Wink Martindale, Jaye P. Morgan, even Paul Hornung (the Green Bay Packer), and many others. In Memphis, I visited Vicki Woodall, the National President of Pat Boone's fan club, and a photo of me with Pat and Vicki appeared later in *16 Magazine*. (After she graduated, Vicki went to Hollywood to be Pat's secretary. Something like that was my ambition; the only alternative I could see was working at the Merit.) When the Hilltoppers played the Michigan State Fair, in Detroit, I appeared with the Hilltoppers on Soupy Sales' original TV show, and I was also interviewed by Robin Seymour and Don McLeod, major DJs on my request list. Johnnie Ray, whose big hits were "Cry" and "The Little White Cloud That Cried," stopped by the Hilltoppers' trailer at the fair one day. He flirted with me and seemed a little reckless, but his show was terrific. On the same bill was

At the Michigan State Fair, summer 1957. I was interviewed by several DJs and was on TV too.

Eydie Gormé—before she married Steve Lawrence and they became Steve and Eydie. Eydie told me she admired my pixie haircut. Some weeks later, I saw her on TV and she had had her hair pixied. And at the Cotton Ball in Blytheville, Arkansas, I met Narvel Felts, a guy with a slick pompadour who said he was a singer in the style of Elvis. He asked for my autograph because I was a National President. More than twenty years later, I heard his name again, on the radio. He had finally made it. He had a hit record.

The day my mother and I drove to Blytheville and met Narvel Felts was the day the Russians sent up Sputnik. After the Hilltoppers' show, Don McGuire drove back to Mayfield with us in our Nash Rambler and then caught a bus to his home in Owensboro. As we rode through the night, listening to Chuck Berry and Little Richard and Elvis Presley on an after-hours show from New Orleans, we were aware of Sputnik spying on us. I noted the Sputnik launch in my diary:

October 4. Blytheville, Ark. Cotton Ball. Hilltoppers and Jimmy
Featherstone Ork. Russian sattelite, Sputnik, launched.
November 3. Sputnik II.
November 7. 40th anniversary of Russian Revolution. President
Eisenhower's address to the nation. Senior rings.
November 15. UFO sightings increase.
December 11. English theme, "National Security." A +.

That fall, when I was a senior, a girl named Janine Williams went with my mother and me to see the Hilltoppers at a ballroom in a little town in Tennessee. Janine was popular at school, and she made a great impression on the Hilltoppers with her teasing, flirtatious personality. All the crinolines she wore under her dress made her look ready for flight, for a trip into outer space. "My brother went to Louisville to the basketball tournament last year," she told the Hilltoppers. "He won the tickets, and he flew up there in an airplane. And he stayed in the same hotel as the teams."

This was an outright lie—I didn't know why she told it—but the Hilltoppers didn't know the difference, so I didn't know what to say. I was happy, though, showing off the Hilltoppers to my friend. Jimmy introduced both of us to the audience at a special moment in the show before they sang "To Be Alone," in which Don did an Ink Spots–style monologue in his surprising bass voice and caused girls to squeal. (He had cherubic looks.) The Hilltoppers had a new record, "Starry Eyes," backed with "You Sure Look Good to Me," but they didn't sing it. I was disappointed. I was afraid it wasn't going to be a hit, and I was getting frustrated with the power of positive thinking. I hadn't told the Hilltoppers about the ESP experiments I had been trying (they involved sending telepathic messages to DJs to play Hilltoppers tunes). I was afraid the Hilltoppers would laugh. I wanted them to think I was normal. One of the fan-club presidents I had visited in Cape Girardeau, Missouri, had a deformed back and didn't even go to school. Another one I knew weighed about three hundred pounds, and her ambition was to be an actress. It was depressing.

"What do you think of Elvis?" Janine asked the Hilltoppers later. Elvis was singing "All Shook Up" on the radio of the Cadillac as Jimmy drove us out to a café for hamburgers.

"He's great," said Sy. "He has a fine voice."

"If I could wiggle like that, we'd make a million dollars," Jimmy said.

Don laughed. "Our manager had a chance once to manage Elvis, but he turned it down. He said nobody with a name like 'Elvis' would get anywhere."

"I like Elvis," Mama said. "He can really carry a tune."

For me, there was something as familiar about Elvis as our farm, with the oak trees and the cows and the chickens. It was as though Elvis were me, listening to WLAC and then coming up with his own songs about the way he felt about the world. I tried not to think too hard about Elvis. Janine had said to me, "If I got Elvis in a dark corner, I'd tear his clothes off."

Janine grew impatient with me and my obsession, and we didn't stay friends. She was going steady with a basketball player I had once had a crush on, and she had no interest in things like flying saucers and reincarnation. I had read *Reincarnation: A Hope of the World*, and it impressed me. I was filled with philosophical questions and I wrote a paper for English class on agnosticism. My teacher, Miss Florence, summoned me to her office and accused me of plagiarism. "Young lady, you have no business entertaining ideas like this," she said. "Where did you get such an idea?"

I quaked. "I read about it. I read lots of philosophy," I said, which was only partly a lie. Reincarnation was philosophy, sort of. I told her I had read John Locke, which *was* a lie. But I hadn't plagiarized. I really believed it was possible that God did not exist, and furthermore it seemed likely that there was no way to know whether he did or not.

Miss Florence had lavender hair, and she kept a handkerchief tucked in her sleeve. Now and then she daintily plucked it out and snuffled into it. She was a terrifying woman, much admired by the whole town. Everyone since the thirties had been in her English class.

"Take my advice," she said, growing softer. "Give up these strange ideas of yours. Your field is mathematics. That's what you're good at. Stay away from these peculiar questions, because they're destructive. And stick with the Bible. That's all the philosophy you'll ever need."

I was silent, rigid with fury—too intimidated to speak.

"You have a lot of big ideas, but they will lead you astray," Miss Florence said in dismissal.

I immersed myself in my presidential duties, publishing my bimonthly newsletter, *Hilltoppers Topics*. In Mayfield, I was an outcast, but in the greater world I was suave and self-important. When DJs interviewed me, I spoke

Jimmy and I were interviewed by Harry Fender, KMOX, St. Louis, on a late-night talk show on CBS Radio.

glibly in *Billboard* lingo. "Well, Ed, this new platter is slated to be a chart-buster," I said to Ed Bonner on KXOK. I had my own stationery, with a Hilltoppers logo. Running a fan club was expensive, but the Hilltoppers sent me ten dollars a week for expenses and fifteen dollars a week for myself. I saved all my money for college. I started hating math.

My mother had been serious about those Tony Martin suits. Shortly before my graduation, the Hilltoppers came to Mayfield, and Mama whisked them off to the Merit and got them measured for the suits. They picked out

The Hilltoppers in Tony Martin jackets.

an off-white material with a subtle gray stripe in it. (Later, when the suits were finished, Mama went to the Merit and personally sewed in the labels.) That spring, I was a soda jerk at the Rexall drugstore in Mayfield, making fifty cents an hour, and after school that day I was drawing a Coke from the fountain for one of the regulars when all four of the Hilltoppers strolled into the drugstore. It was my big moment: I could show them off. A classmate of mine, one of those popular cheerleaders—an uptown girl who had made me feel like a shabby bumpkin—was testing nail polish at the cosmetics counter. I rushed over and told her I would introduce her to the Hilltoppers. "They're here," I said, pointing to the end of the counter, where I had served them Cokes.

"Oh, I don't think so," she said, flashing her cheerleader smile. "I wouldn't know what to say." With two fingernails painted Persian Melon, she hurried out the back door of the drugstore. The Hilltoppers scared her.

It was a triumph, sort of. I got off work early, and the Hilltoppers drove me home in the Cadillac. Mama made a huge catfish supper, with hush puppies and slaw and blackberry pie, and that evening my family and I all went to Paducah and saw the Hilltoppers sing at the National Guard Armory with Blue Barron's orchestra. It was a perfect day. "Your mother is an amazing woman," Don said to me.

The Hilltoppers were so conventional, such nice guys. I didn't know how to talk to them about the crazy thoughts in my head. I had just received a reply to my letter to George Adamski, the man who claimed in his book

The Hilltoppers at my house in Kentucky.

about UFOs to have been on a spaceship to Venus. He thanked me for writing and assured me that he had indeed been to Venus, but he failed to answer my questions about the spacecraft's interior and the landscape of Venus.

That summer, I picked blackberries in the early-morning dew with rock-and-roll songs like "Get a Job" by the Silhouettes and Eddie Cochran's "Summertime Blues" blasting in my mind, and in the afternoons I trudged down the dusty lanes through the fields with the dog to round up the herd of cows. In the evenings, I worked at the Rexall. I went out with boys—boys who wanted to settle down and work in the new factories—but I wasn't impressed. I was always dreaming. Our house was close to Highway 45, which ran straight south to Tupelo, Mississippi, where Elvis was born. I knew he had dreamed the same dreams.

Miss Florence refused to write me a recommendation to Duke University, where I wanted to study parapsychology with the famous Dr. J. B. Rhine, so in the fall I went away to the University of Kentucky, in Lexington, where I fell in love with a boy who was interested in UFOs and mind expansion. He wrote a column for the college newspaper and had a sense of humor that reminded me of Max Shulman's *Rally Round the Flag, Boys!* I neglected my fan-club duties and failed to get *Hilltoppers Topics* out on schedule. All the mysteries of the universe lay before me, and I couldn't learn fast enough. I read *Brave New World* and *1984* and *On the Beach* and *Mandingo* and *Elmer Gantry*. I studied French and psychology and philosophy and volleyball. After hours, I still listened to John R jive-talking along with Ruth Brown and Little Walter and Jimmy Reed. Buddy Holly died that winter. Elvis was in the Army.

Earlier in the school year, before I fell in love, the Hilltoppers played at homecoming, and I went to the dance without a date—an unheard-of thing for a girl to do in those days. But I wouldn't have missed their show. I never tired of seeing it—even the old comic bit when the guys rolled up Don's pantlegs without his knowledge while he was singing the solo of "Ka-Ding-Dong." They always opened with something fast-paced, like "I Can't Give You Anything but Love" or "I've Got the World on a String," and sometimes they followed up with "Toot Toot Tootsie (Goo' Bye)"—which Jimmy sang as "Toot Toot *Tootie*"—before launching into their own numbers. Jimmy was noted for his clumsy introductions: "Ladies and gentleman, and now we want to do the song that you made possible our being here with by buying those . . ." That night, as he always did when I was at their show, Jimmy introduced me to the audience, and the spotlight hit my face, momentarily blinding me. This time, I was embarrassed, because I thought everyone there would know I didn't have a date and would think I was peculiar. I felt as though I had just arrived from the moon.

The curfew was extended to 2 A.M. that night, because the Hilltoppers' show was late, and Sy walked me to my dorm. We sat in the parlor, surrounded by sorority pledges and their anxious dates. Some of them stared at us. Sy was the only one in the room in a tuxedo. I was the only one in the room who seemed to have a date with a member of the famous singing group that had just performed at the big dance. The lights in the parlor were bright, and the elderly housemother patrolled nervously. I got a fit of giggles when she looked at Sy suspiciously, as though he might be secretly organizing a panty raid. She had drilled the dorm residents in the horrors of panty raids, making them seem something like acts of terrorism.

A year later, I saw the Hilltoppers for the last time, at a night club in Louisville, where they were performing with Mel Tormé. I had driven over with some girls from U.K. The Hilltoppers' popularity had declined drastically. It wasn't my fault, though. They were being eclipsed by rock and roll. In their tuxedos or in their Tony Martin suits, they never really got the hang of it. That night in Louisville, I remember Don and Sy sitting at a table in a corner with me. They were as kind as ever—funny and generous, the way I always remember them. I had on a black cocktail dress with a taffeta balloon hem. "Those U.K. boys better watch out," Don said, teasing me.

Shyly, I told them about my boyfriend. By then, he was going with some other girl and my life was in ruins, but I didn't go into detail. I apologized for letting my club work slip. The newsletter was two months late.

Don smiled. "It's about time you forgot about the fan club," he said.

"No, it's not," I said loyally.

"You'll have other interests," he said. "You'll get married, and have your own family."

"I don't know." I knew I could never love anyone but that boy with the sense of humor. I would never get married.

"People change and go on to something else," Don said. "We won't stay with this forever. It's no way to live—one dinky ballroom after another. Traveling around all the time isn't what it's cracked up to be."

"Even in a Cadillac?" I asked.

"Even in a Cadillac," Don said, smiling again. "By the way, we'll drop you off in Lexington tomorrow."

"Thank you," I said. It was my last chance to travel in their Cadillac, I thought—a good way to end my national presidency. They had traded in the blue Cadillac for a newer, black model. I imagine it even now, rushing through the night, unrestrained in its flight, charging across America.

It was after midnight that night when Mel Tormé finished his set, but the band wouldn't quit. The crowd was wild. Jimmy took the microphone again. He sang "I Can't Get Started," a droopy-drawers sort of song. He had had a couple of drinks, and he was in mellow spirits. Then he eased into "St. James Infirmary." As the deep sadness of the song emerged, he suddenly became real to me, not a star. "St. James Infirmary" was slow and bluesy, but it wasn't a droopy-drawers song. It was the meanest, low-downest, saddest song I ever heard. I thought I would die. It was after hours, way down South in Dixie. It was 1959.

The Hilltoppers rode their behemoth Cadillac and played one-night stands only a while longer. Sy worked in a tobacco warehouse for a time, and then he and Jimmy became sales representatives for Dot Records. Don settled in Lexington. I lost touch with them. In the seventies, during the nostalgia rage, I heard that Jimmy Sacca was on the road again with a new Hilltoppers group. After college, in the sixties, I went to New York and got a job writing for a fan magazine—the same magazine that had once listed my fan club in its Betty Burr column. I found out that Betty Burr, who had once been an honorary member of my club, was only a name, like Miss Lonelyhearts. Part of my job at the fan mag was to write Betty Burr columns about fan clubs. I did that for about a year, and after that I left New York.

GOING UP

TO ATLANTA

JAMES ALAN McPHERSON

This is the only picture I have of my father. It was taken sometime in the 1930s, at his mother's family home in Hardeeville, South Carolina, when he was a young man. I have known all along that he liked comic books. Someone has pointed out to me that he is wearing a down jacket. The wearing of down jackets did not become fashionable until many years after this picture was taken. But a down jacket would be most comfortable during the cool, rainy winters that settle into the coastal areas of Georgia and South Carolina. My father's roots were in this region. Knowing its climate, he must have dressed with an eye toward comfort.

Someone else has noted that he seems arrogant. I cannot remember him this way, although some arrogance, for him, was possible. But most likely his arms are crossed and his eyes are closed and his head is tilted because he is asleep. I have learned that he suffered from narcolepsy, an inherited disorder that causes a person to fall asleep at absolutely any time. My brother, Richard, inherited this condition from my father. I note that my father has small hands. This is surprising, considering the fact that he labored all his life as an electrician. I want to believe that he was not fated to be a laborer.

When my father died, in late December 1961, I had just returned to Savannah from Morris Brown College in Atlanta. In my own mind, my father had died many years before. I attended the funeral, but grew angry when the Methodist minister who conducted the services said, "We all knew Mac, and we all know he's better off where he is now."

I did not attend the burial.

James Allen McPherson, Sr. 1913–1961.

James Alan McPherson

Moving Pictures

In California, many years ago, I saw a Japanese film called *Sansho the Bailiff*. The film is about Japan during its Middle Ages, when slavery existed as an institution. It tells the story of a family.

The Governor of a certain province, who is an aristocrat, decides on his own that human slavery is wrong. He decrees its abolition. But the decree threatens the human property of Sansho the Bailiff, who is the most powerful slaveholder in the province. The Shogun immediately revokes the Governor's decree, because it threatens to undermine the social order, and transfers the offending Governor to a remote province, where his personal feelings about slavery will pose no threat. The departing Governor sends his family, a wife and two children, to live with her parents. While traveling, they are kidnapped by slave traders. The mother is sold into prostitution. The two children are sold to Sansho the Bailiff. They grow up as slaves. The son becomes dehumanized and loses his memory of his former life and therefore his identity. He becomes such a good slave that he is promoted to the rank of trustee. It becomes his job to mutilate, kill or bury any slave who tries to escape or who dies of work or of old age. During one trip outside the slave compound, a very beautiful thing happens. The young man and his sister are gathering branches in order to bury an old woman. They have to break some branches from trees. They both pull at a branch together. It breaks and they fall down. The fall is a repetition of a similar fall they had, as children, when they were gathering branches for a fire the night the family was captured by slave traders. This ritual gesture, recalling the last happy moment they shared before becoming slaves, revives the young man's former psychological habits. He begins, slowly, to reclaim himself. His sister, at the sacrifice of her own life, eventually helps him to escape. He eludes the slave catchers and, after great difficulty, petitions the Shogun to restore his family name. Recognizing the offspring of his former official, the Shogun makes the young man Governor of the province. He now occupies the same position as his father, who by now is dead. The son immediately issues a decree outlawing slavery. Whereas his father, an aristocrat, had outlawed slavery out of his own intuitive distaste for the institution, the son, having been a slave, has an *earned* contempt for the dehumanizing aspects of the institution. Even though his sister is dead and his mother is now an aged, mutilated prostitute, the son does achieve the father's original desire. But he achieves it for reasons that are personally and emotionally sound.

He *learns.*

I learned from this film that, among the Asians, the offspring can ennoble the ancestor.

In Atlanta

My father's half brother, Thomas McPherson, Jr., is closer to my age than he is to my father's. He was born, during my grandfather's second marriage, after my father had achieved adulthood. James Allen McPherson, Sr., my father, was himself like a father to Thomas McPherson, Jr.

In the late 1960s, Thomas, a trained minister, became District Director of the Equal Employment Opportunity Commission. His office in Atlanta covered Georgia, South Carolina and Alabama. I visited him there once and met some of his employees. One especially cheerful older white man was very pleased to meet me. His name was Bill Harris. My uncle Thomas introduced us, and explained that Bill Harris, because he was once Sheriff of Chatham County, Georgia (which included Savannah), once knew my father very well. Bill Harris had arrested my father many times, not for any personal offense but for "cheating and swindling," for not completing work he had contracted to do. Bill Harris shook my hand and said, "Everybody liked Mac. It's just that he couldn't hold his liquor."

I remembered Bill Harris. I remembered one night he came to our house to arrest my father. I was about six. My father had come home to say good-bye to us. His ambition had always been to go up to Atlanta and start over. He had come to see us one last time before he left Savannah. We lived on the top floor of a duplex at 509½ West Walburg Street. It was a cool winter night, in December, and we had no lights or heat except for the fireplace in the bedroom. For light we used candles and an oil lamp. I remember the four of us, and my mother, standing at the top of the stairs. Mary, my older sister, was holding the lamp. All of us were crying while my father said good-bye. Just as he turned to walk down the stairs, the front door opened and Bill Harris, the Sheriff of Chatham County, came in the door and said, "All right, Mac, get your hat."

I think now that if he had not loved us enough to come to the house to say good-bye, he would have gotten away.

Augusta

Thomas McPherson, Sr., my grandfather, lived at 1635 15th Street in Augusta. I associate Augusta with Christmas.

Thomas McPherson, Sr., was for most of his life an insurance salesman for Guaranty Life Insurance Company. He married twice. His first marriage was to Alice Scarborough of Hardeeville, South Carolina. That marriage lasted until shortly after my father was born. His second marriage, when he was in middle age, was to Josephine Martin of Blackshare, Georgia. She was my mother's first cousin. By this marriage he had two children, Thomas and Eva, and moved from Savannah to Augusta. There he led a poor but respectable life. In Savannah, we lived almost always in poverty: public welfare, clothes from the Salvation Army, no lights or heat for years at a time, double sessions in the segregated public schools, work at every possible job that would pay the bills. Each year at Christmas, if my father was not with us, my grandfather would try to arrange to bring us to Augusta, so we could share the family Christmas at his home. Sometimes we would go by train. Other times he would try to arrange a ride for the four of us with the insurance men with whom he worked. I can't remember whether or not my grandfather owned a car.

When I think about Augusta, I remember ambrosia. It was made with coconuts, apples, pecans, oranges and lots of spices. It would be served with Christmas dinner, late at night, when people would not notice the small amounts of food. But in the mornings, there was the anticipation of toys. Sometimes we would get old toys that had been repaired by Thomas and Eva. Thomas had a chicken coop in their backyard, and he liked to show me how, with the sound of his voice, he had trained the chickens to cut off and on, off and on, the light in their coop. He had a bicycle, and would take time to ride me on the back seat of it before he went to work. Once, when I had a very bad cold, Thomas bought a lemon for me. I remember that lemon after all these years because the gesture was grounded in love.

I also remember my grandfather, who had a nervous condition, sitting at the head of the table and moving his hands up and down, up and down, to steady his nerves. After the meal, which was the high point of Christmas Day, he would say to his wife, "Joe, I enjoyed the meal." And she would answer, "I'm glad you did, Mr. Mac." Afterwards, before it was time to go to bed, I would sit alone in the living room and draw Christmas trees. I had, then, great talent as a drawer of Christmas trees. I still love trains because sometimes we would take the Nancy Hanks, run by the Georgia Central Line, from Savannah to Augusta.

Janie McPherson
"Aunt China"

Whenever I ran away, I would get as far as Aunt China's house. I would say, "Aunt China, I'm running away." She would look severely at me and say, "What's wrong with you, boy? Here, sit down and eat some of these greens and rice." I loved Aunt China. She was the wife of Robert McPherson, my grandfather's brother, and lived on West 32nd Street in Savannah. I think she was pure African.

My Uncle Bob, Robert McPherson, was only one of my grandfather's brothers. The others were Joe, B.J. and George. My Uncle George, whom I never met, was a Presiding Elder in the African Methodist Episcopal Church. The family agreed that he could preach the fuzz off a Georgia peach. Uncle Bob and Aunt China were like parents to my father. I think now that he must have run away to their house many times, even after he was a full-grown man. I know that, when I was a boy, I could always find out where he was if I went there.

Aunt China was a very strong woman. She never asked "real" questions, but seemed to know everything. She seemed never bothered by anything in life. All of us leaned on her, absorbed her strength. She seemed to assume that everything in life could be cured by a good meal and a good night's sleep. I liked to go there when I ran away.

Several days before my father died, he sent word that he wanted to see me. He had been living in a rented room in 33rd Lane, just a few blocks away from Aunt China's house. I did not go to see him. But when the news came that he was dead, I ran away to Aunt China's. This was one of the few days when she was not at home. I was making up my mind to go on to the rooming house where my father had just died, and I was walking down 32nd Lane, when I saw Aunt China coming up the lane toward me. Down the lane, in the distance behind her, I could see an ambulance loading my father's body. It was the only time I ever saw my Aunt China cry. She took me home with her and kept crying and saying, "*I told that fool. I told that boy.*"

James Alan McPherson

Houses

The stable houses were Aunt China's on 32nd Street and wherever my Aunt Beulah Collins was, anyplace in Savannah. The others were places we lived.

We lived at 509½ West Walburg Street, next door to a funeral parlor, from the time I was born until 1951. Then we moved to 2010 West Bulloch Street and lived there until 1953. Then we moved to Green Cove Springs, Florida, for a summer. Then we moved back to Savannah and lived there with our cousin, Cassie Harper, until 1955. Then we moved to the east side of town, into a small apartment at 508 East Henry Street. In 1957 we moved to 1006½ Montgomery Street, into a duplex owned by an electrician named T. J. Hopkins. We lived there until 1960. Then we moved to 316 West Hall Street, about five blocks away. In 1963 my mother moved into a housing project named Catton Homes.

During all this time, I liked Aunt China's house the best. I could always go there from the other places. Of the other places, I liked the duplex on Montgomery Street the best. The adjoining apartment was vacant, and I could get into it through a hole in the closet of one of the bedrooms. I liked to crawl through that hole, sit on the floor in the empty, quiet apartment and be alone.

Ebony, North Carolina
Eva McPherson (Clayton)

In 1980, I went to North Carolina to see Eva, my father's half sister. She is a very successful woman and was, at that time, a County Commissioner. Except for brief exchanges at funerals, I had not seen her since I was a child.

I asked Eva about my father. She told me that he was considered a "brain." She said that, in his day, he was the only licensed black master electrician in the entire state of Georgia. I asked her what had happened to him. She said she did not know. I asked her whether he chased women. She said that he was a faithful husband, but liked to drink and gamble. She said his only real love was electricity. She said that he had invented a device once that, when placed over an outlet, would reduce the *cost*, but not the flow, of electricity.

She said that the officials threatened to take away his license if he ever tried to market it. She said that I was not the first in my immediate family to attend college. She said that my father had attended the same college I finished, Morris Brown College in Atlanta, but had been expelled after the first semester for gambling. She said that, during World War II, he had been deferred from active service because he taught a course at Savannah State College, a course in engineering, that was considered essential. She said that he was a completely self-taught man, having never attended any grade beyond one college semester. I asked Eva how it was that such a gifted man could wind up dying of frost exposure in a rented room in a dirt lane in Savannah. Eva said she did not know.

I told Eva that I believed my father had been frustrated by having his license taken from him and by having to work for an older man, T. J. Hopkins, as a common electrician. I told her that I believed that my father had considered Hopkins a father-substitute, against whom he was always rebelling. Eva said this was inaccurate. She said that the older man, Hopkins, had been my father's student. She said that Mr. Hopkins had never been a master electrician, only a licensed one, and that my father had never wanted to work for him. She said that his ambition, always, had been to start his own company in Savannah or in Atlanta. I asked her why I had never been told these things.

Eva said she did not know.

Samuel James Collins, Jr.
"Bro"

Sam Collins is the oldest son of Beulah Collins, my mother's sister. It was Beulah Collins who drew my mother out of Green Cove Springs, Florida, and into Savannah. Beulah had left Green Cove Springs to marry a man named Samuel Collins who lived in Savannah. He was an ice-man by trade. He sent so many letters to Mary Smalls, my mother's mother, back in Green Cove Springs, letters that kept reciting the line "Beulah and me is having a wonderful time. We eat collard greens every day," that Mary Smalls became suspicious. She sent my mother, the oldest daughter, into Savannah to see about Beulah. While there she lived with her first cousin, Josephine Martin, who had just married a man named Thomas McPherson, Sr. James

McPherson, the grown son of my mother's cousin's new husband, was sitting around the house reading comic books. My mother never went back to Green Cove Springs.

Samuel and Beulah Collins had four children: Barbara and Lucille, Sam and Harry. When we were growing up we were as close as brothers and sisters. I loved their mother with them. There was always laughter and life in their house. Sometimes, at Thanksgiving or at Christmas, when we had nothing to eat, Beulah would steal a can of mackerel for us from the family for whom she worked. My mother would make mackerel croquettes. But the best things about my Aunt Beulah's house were the magical things that happened on weekends. I would go there on Friday evenings and would not have to leave until Sunday night. Bro would tell me some of the things I could not have learned on my own.

We were not as close after we became adolescents. I had to work all the time, and go to school. My world was made up of school and jobs and reading. Bro moved into the street culture. In this way, through word of mouth, he came to know my father much better than I did. He joined the group of men who stood around the fire on the corner of Anderson and 31st streets. My father was also part of that group.

Years later, Samuel Collins told me that the men around the fire used to call my father "Papasqualli," their version of a Creek or Cherokee word meaning "Chief." He said that whenever the men had an argument, before they came to blows over the issue in dispute, one of them would say, "Well, let's go ask Mac." He said my father would delight the men around the fire with his command of language. He would say things like, "I think I shall repair to the bathroom." Samuel Collins said that, once, when one of the men said something negative about my mother, my father picked him up and threw him into the fire. He said that, usually, my father was a gentle man.

T. J. Hopkins

Called "Major" publicly by influential people in the white community, Mr. Hopkins was the only other licensed electrician in Savannah who was black. He had served in the U.S. Army, had attended school. He was always willing to employ my father, to give him a job as a common electrician. Once, after my father had gotten out of prison and had resumed working for him, Mr. Hopkins rented my father an apartment in his duplex just over the office of his company at 2010 Montgomery Street. My father had only to go downstairs to work and back upstairs to his family. Mr. Hopkins even allowed my brother and me to work for him, sorting electrical parts and cleaning out his office. In this way we could help our father pay off the rent. Nights, Mr. Hopkins sat at the main desk in his office talking on the telephone. Seated in the white glare of the neon lights, he looked, to anyone watching through the plate-glass window, like an actor on stage.

But my father was always losing his temper and quitting the job. His ambition was to regain his old license as a master electrician and start his own company. He had tried this many times and had always failed. Many of the men who worked for Hopkins were former members of my father's old crews. They were still loyal to him. Sometimes, a few of them would quit when he quit, and would not go back until *he* was forced, by family pressures, to go back. Mr. Hopkins was always willing to take him back.

But my father's ambition, always, was to regain his license and then go up to Atlanta, where he could start his own company.

Reidsville

The people at Reidsville would always welcome my father back. He was not a criminal, but many of the hardened criminals there loved him. My father was a great cook, and was always assigned to the kitchen. I think he was considered too valuable to waste on the road gang.

We used to go from Savannah to Reidsville to see my father. I was always very ashamed to see him come into the visiting room because there was a wire screen between him and us. But at the same time I was glad to see him. We always wore our best clothes when we went to Reidsville. My father, because he worked in the kitchen, gained weight there. He was always healthier after he had settled into the routine of prison life. But during one of his last stays, they gave him electric shock treatments. When he came back to Savannah, after that time, he went back to work for Hopkins without complaining. But he began to drink almost all the time. Sometime after that, when I was twelve or thirteen, I stopped trying to see him. If I saw him on Anderson Street after school, I would turn and walk the other way.

The last time I saw my father alive, I was seventeen. I had gotten a National Defense Student Loan and was about to go to college in Atlanta. I went looking for him one night and found him, standing by the fire, on the corner of Anderson and 31st streets. I had, by this time, been working every possible kind of job to help support the family I thought he had abandoned. During all my years in Savannah, I had never had peace or comfort or any chance to rely on anyone else. I blamed him for it. I was very bitter toward him. That night I lectured him, telling him to straighten himself out, as I had, and be a man. He said he was hungry and wanted something to eat. I bought a meal for him with money I had earned on my own. After he had eaten it he said to me, "And a little child shall lead them."

This was the last thing he ever said to me.

Hardeeville, South Carolina
Eliza Moore

Mary and I drove from Virginia to Savannah in late 1980 to see about our mother. On the way back, we stopped off in Hardeeville, South Carolina, to see our aunt, Eliza Moore. She was my father's aunt, the sister of his mother, Alice Scarborough. After my grandfather and her sister divorced, Aunt Liza grew embittered toward our family. We never knew the reasons.

When we walked into the house she said, "You look just like James McPherson." Later, she brought out a number of pictures she had been saving for years. She gave me a picture of my father. She showed us pictures of Alice Scarborough. My grandmother was very beautiful. In every picture she was elegantly dressed. Her second husband, the man she married after my grandfather, was also elegantly dressed. Alice Scarborough was a mulatto. Aunt Liza explained that her family had been in Hardeeville since long before the Civil War. She gave me the ancestral names: Scarborough, Strains and Wattley. She said that some of the white descendants of these families still lived in Hardeeville. She told me that we had small shares in the property on which she lived. She said that James McPherson had been recognized as a "brain." She did not know what happened to him, although she had her suspicions.

Alice Scarborough.

James Alan McPherson

Green Cove Springs, Florida, 1953
John Smalls

My one memory of my mother's father is of him sitting in a wheel-chair on the porch of his home in Green Cove Springs. He was tall and thin and stern-faced, and was squeezing two red rubber balls. He was, at that time, recovering from a stroke. My mother presented each of her four children to him as we walked up the steps. He asked each of us our names. When I said, "My name is James Allen McPherson, Jr.," he looked down at me and said, "You are not welcome here."

John Smalls had been a sharecropper in Blackshare, Georgia, when my mother was born. Before that, he had apparently moved between Florida, South Carolina and Georgia, working on plantations. He had two sons and five daughters: Bill, Joe, Mable, Beulah, Martha, Mary, Suzie. My mother, Mable, was the oldest of his five girls. My aunt Suzie, who now lives in Detroit, maintains that one of her father's uncles, Robert Smalls, was a Representative from South Carolina in the U.S. Congress during the Reconstruction. She maintains that she has a book about his life. My mother has consistently denied this. She has never talked much about her background.

Both John Smalls and his wife, Mary, were of the Seminole people. Their ancestors were the runaway slaves and free black people and Creek and Cherokee who fled to the Florida swamps, in the early nineteenth century, to form their own nation. There, they continued their struggle for freedom. The U.S. government finally surrendered to the Seminole people in the early 1970s.

My mother told me that, when he was a sharecropper in Blackshare, Georgia, my grandfather was given the job of a white overseer. The owner of the plantation fired him. The former overseer swore he would come around and kill my grandfather. My mother said that she was a child then, and could remember her father sitting all night on the porch of their house, with a shotgun on his knee, waiting for the white man to come back. Since then, I think, my mother has always run away from trouble.

When I met him that summer in Green Cove Springs, John Smalls was the wealthiest black man in town. He owned several farms, a general store, a service station, and a number of houses. I don't know how he acquired this wealth, but I believe he worked very hard for it. My mother's mother, Mary, had died some years before, and my grandfather's second wife, Miss Annie, was in charge of his health and his property. I think she must have felt threatened by my mother and the four children she had brought home from Savannah. We had been evicted from our apartment, our furniture had been repossessed, our parents were separated, and we had no place else to go. Almost every week that summer my grandfather would say he wanted to go into Jacksonville so he could change his will. Miss Annie never set a date for the car trip. Finally, my mother left us in Green Cove Springs and went back to Savannah. She got a job as a domestic and a room for the five of us with her cousin, Cassie Harper. Then she came back and got us.

My grandfather never changed his will. When he died Miss Annie inherited all the property. My mother and her sisters never insisted on shares in the property. A few years later, Miss Annie sold all the assets and moved to New York.

Cousin Cassie Harper, 1954

I think that the happiest time of my life was when my mother returned to Green Cove Springs to get us and took us back to Savannah. I remember the five of us walking, one summer night, from the bus station on West Broad Street all the way to West 44th Street. I remember we were walking across a park to Cousin Cassie's house. We were holding hands. I think we sang. We sang songs we had learned at St. Mary's School and in Augusta. The trees were flush with thick green leaves lighted by the white moonlight. There was the scent of wisteria in everything. The whole park was dark and light and purple and green and thick-scented. The sky was absolutely clear and starry. I *know* we were singing.

Cousin Cassie's house was at 711 West 44th Street, in the middle-class section of the black community. We rented one bedroom, but were told that we had use of the entire house. Above us, on the top floor of the duplex, a woman named Sadie Stevens lived with Helene and Alreatha, her two daughters. There was a front porch with a swing. I liked to sit on the swing with Helene and sing popular songs to her. On our left lived Reverend Moore and his six children. They had a television set, and if I sat on the swing while their door was open I could watch whatever was on television. I especially liked Saturday and Sunday nights, when "The Toast of the Town" and "Walt Disney Presents" came on.

Cousin Cassie, though, was an embittered woman. She was a mulatto and had long gray-black hair that she liked to plait in two long braids while sitting on the edge of her bed. She always wore a flowing pink nightgown because she had severe arthritis that made it difficult for her to move. She had to spend almost all of her time in bed, and when she did walk it was with crutches. Root doctors in South Carolina had advised her that certain kinds of worms, fried and made into a salve, would relieve her pain. She had a huge skillet in which she fried worms almost all the time. She also had a great number of cats. Sometimes Cousin Cassie could be very sweet. Other times she was very mean. During the times when she was being mean, when we lived there, we did not go out of our room.

The five of us slept in the bedroom. My brother and sisters and I slept on one bed, while my mother slept on a cot across the room. We considered that room our home and did not take the rest of the house for granted. We were very careful to stay in our room when Cousin Cassie was being mean. We could tell she was being mean if we heard her coming down the hall kicking her cats out of the way with her crutches. No matter what she did or said to us, while our mother was at work, she would always try to make peace with us children before our mother came home. She would say, "We're all here together." And she would suggest that we go into the living room the next Sunday and pray together. We did this any number of times.

Cousin Cassie had an agreement with a man named Mr. Sellers, who was not very bright and who was totally alone in the world. In exchange for his wages from his work as a longshoreman, she agreed to cook meals for him. Most often my family and I did most of the cooking, except when Cousin Cassie insisted on serving him mutton. When she wanted to cook mutton we let her do it herself, because we could not stand the smell of mutton. It tended to linger in all the rooms of the house.

Cousin Cassie owned a number of houses on West 44th Street, and a number of houses in the lane behind it, and a lot of land in South Carolina. All of her relatives deferred to her. She had another agreement with Mrs. Eloise George, a niece who lived in one of her houses just next door to the one in which we lived. It was agreed that whenever Cousin Cassie needed something she would knock on the wall of Eloise's house and the niece would come over to help. In exchange for this, Cousin Cassie promised Eloise to leave her a considerable part of her property. Although this was the agreement, my family and Mr. Sellers did all the work for Cousin Cassie. We did it because we loved her, or were dependent on her, or were frightened of her.

During this time my grandfather, Thomas McPherson, Sr., died, and my mother developed an extreme case of ulcers. She was unable to work and would lie in bed, day and night, spitting up blood and in the most extreme pain. We thought she would die, too. She could not go to my grandfather's funeral. A guard brought my father in handcuffs from Reidsville. I watched the guard unlock the handcuffs so my father could approach his father's grave. Afterwards, the guard brought my father to Cousin Cassie's house so he could see my mother before going back to Reidsville. My father saw my mother moaning on her cot in our room and he began to cry.

When Cousin Cassie died, her niece Eloise and her brother began fighting over the property. This was what Cousin Cassie had wanted all along. She had always told us, "I'm not making a will for the dogs. When I die, I want them to fight over it." They fought for years. Both the niece and the brother approached my mother and promised her a house if she would testify, in court, for one or the other of them. My mother refused. The four of us—my sisters, my brother and me—pleaded with her to testify for *someone*, even though we knew that we had done all the work for Cousin Cassie, because we wanted to have a house of our own. My mother refused even us. Lawyers finally got all the property, through the manipulations at which they are so skillful.

But a few years before Cousin Cassie died, my father came out of Reidsville again. He moved us into a small apartment on East Henry Street. He went back to work for T. J. Hopkins.

Dr. E. J. Smith
("Imhotep")

Dr. Smith delivered my sisters, my brother and me. Then he stepped back and watched us grow up. He and his wife had no children of their own, so he must have loved all the children he delivered. During his entire life, he never let go of us.

When we lived with Cousin Cassie on West 44th Street, he stepped back into our lives. He and his wife lived on West 41st Street, only three or four blocks away. He began inviting my brother and me around to his house on Saturday mornings. We were paid one quarter each to rake his lawn and clear it of dog shit. But the work assignment was only a ploy. Most of the time with him was spent drinking Postum in his kitchen. During these sessions he would drill into us the details of how he had worked his way through college, and then through medical school, as a waiter. He liked to recite the orders he had to call into the kitchen of the hotel in which he worked. He liked to shout, *"One order of mulligatawny!"* When we drank Postum, the three of us would toast our coffee mugs when Dr. Smith recited to Richard and me:

> We've hit the trail together . . . You and I.
> We've bucked all kinds of wind and weather . . . You and I.
> Although the years may bring success,
> We'll know no greater happiness
> Than knowing we have stood the test
>   OF FRIENDSHIP (click)
>   You and I.

When I was ten or eleven, Dr. Smith took Richard and me down to the offices of the *Savannah Morning News*, the local paper, and asked that they give us jobs. He was told that we could have paper routes if we had bicycles. We had no bicycles. Dr. Smith took us to the Salvation Army Store, on West Henry Street, and bought two used bicycles for us. He then took us back to the offices of the *Savannah Morning News* and got jobs for us. We carried papers for years after that. When my bicycle was stolen, I carried them on my back.

When I was in college I thought a lot about Dr. Smith. By this time I was working, in Atlanta, as a waiter. I kept wanting to shout, *"One order of mulligatawny!"* But I never did. Instead, I returned to Savannah and went to see Dr. and Mrs. Smith. By this time he was old and sick, and did not seem to recognize me. I tried to give him back the money he had paid for the bicycles. He and his wife refused to accept it.

Comic Books

Like my father, I loved comic books. I think he must have introduced me to them. He knew a man, a white man, in Savannah, who ran a wholesale house specializing in comic books. The man must have been one of his customers. Sometimes, my father would take my brother and me there, and the man would let us climb into a huge bin full of remaindered comic books. We would "swim" in the bin full of old comics. The man would let us take as many as we wanted. I always liked the older ones. I remember "Buffalo Bug" because the dialogue was always in verse. I liked "Captain Marvel" and "Batman" and "Superman" and some of the detective ones. I liked "Little Lulu," too, because the last section was a serial about Little Lulu's adventures with an old woman named Witch Hazel. I liked the old "Tarzan" because it also had a serial called "Brothers of the Spear." I did not like the horror comics.

When we lived on East Henry Street, I used to play hooky from school and walk down to the Salvation Army Store on West Henry Street to see if they had any new old comics. Sometimes I would be able to buy them two or three for a nickel. I especially liked the fifty-two pagers, because they provided more story for my money. Over the years, I collected well over seven hundred comic books. I spent so much time at the Salvation Army, wandered up and down its rows so much, that I was considered a regular customer. The old white men who sat in the store, the bums and alcoholics, liked to see me come in because they knew where I would be going. If there were no new old comics, I would look at the books on the shelves next to the cardboard boxes of comic books. One day, I saw a leather-bound edition of the stories of Guy de Maupassant. A teacher at school, a woman named Kay Frances Stripling, had mentioned a story by Maupassant in our English class, and I saw it in the book. I think I paid a dime for a leather-bound edition of Maupassant's stories. I began to read them.

But I still liked comic books. Since I no longer had any interest in school, I would make every possible excuse to not get up in the morning. When my brother and sister had left the house for school, I would wander around town, looking for comic books. Once, I went into a drugstore a few blocks from our apartment and saw a rack full of new comic books. I wanted one of them, but did not have enough money. The comic book rack was near an enclosed telephone booth. I went into the booth and reached my hand out and took several comic books off the rack, and pulled them into the booth. I closed the door and wrapped the comic books around my ankles, over my socks but under the cuffs of my pants. Then I opened the door of the telephone booth and walked out of the store. I walked as casually as possible back to our apartment, and then hid in the closet for well over an hour. Then I tried to read the comics I had stolen. I could not read them. I finally wrapped the comics around my ankles, this time beneath my socks, and walked back to the drugstore. I went into the telephone booth and left them there. Then I walked out of the store again. I never went back into that drugstore for as long as I lived in Savannah. But soon after that, I began going to the Colored Branch of the Carnegie Public Library, up the block from our apartment on East Henry Street, and I would sit there all day reading books at random. When it was time for my brother and sisters to come home from school, I would go back to the house and cook a meal for them.

At one time, I had well over seven hundred comic books.

Affluence

Mary remembers that we were among the first black families in Savannah to have an electric stove. We also had a maid, a woman named Delphene, who used to help our mother with us and who used to give us baths. Mary also remembers that, at one time, my father had his own company and his own truck. It had painted on it: "McPherson & Company: Electrical Contractor." Mary also remembers that our father always gave us money when he came home from work on Fridays. She said that all the kids in the neighborhood would be waiting with us for him to come home. He always gave everyone a share of his earnings. But he would do it by ages, giving the older children more money. Mary said it did not seem to matter to him that his own children expected the best treatment. I do not remember these things. I remember, though, that my father always wanted a street in Savannah named for him.

I also remember attending the best school for "colored" children in the city of Savannah. It was St. Mary's, a Catholic school, on West 36th Street. All the teachers were white nuns. All the students were black. If you talked at St. Mary's when the nuns were out of the room, one of their spies would report you when they came back. Then the talkers had to hold out their palms so the nuns could smack them with a ruler. I never talked. I learned to read very quietly. I was never smacked.

My father always did more than anyone else to support the shows and parties that were put on at St. Mary's. He had a friend named Mr. Simon, a white man who ran an ice-cream plant. My father would always take my brother and me there to pick up five- and ten-gallon cartons of ice cream for the shows at St. Mary's. I think that Mr. Simon had affection for my father. They would always embrace when he went in there. The nuns were very happy to have the free ice cream. My sister, Mary, was always a star in the show.

During my three years at St. Mary's, I was trained to be a Catholic. Mary and Richard and I learned the rosary, attended mass, lit candles. But toward the end of my third year, the priest in charge of St. Mary's called us out of class and into his office. He told us that our father had not paid our tuition for some time, but that since we were such good students he was going to pay it himself. He pulled a wad of money out of his pocket and showed it to us.

I never knew whether my father paid what was owed to St. Mary's. Toward the end of my third year, and my sister's fourth, we were transferred from St. Mary's to the Florence Street School. The black children there had to attend double sessions: half went from early in the morning until noon, and the others went from early afternoon until five or six o'clock. I was put into group five, among the retarded people, during the last part of third grade and through all of fourth. I sat at my desk and never said a word. I read my sister's fifth-grade books on the sly.

Paulson Street School

After we moved to East Henry Street, I had to attend Paulson Street School. This was where all the mean people went. They would throw rocks at you, push you in the halls, trying to make you fight. I did not want to fight anyone. During the years at Paulson we were eligible for the free lunch program. This was available, through the state, for anyone on public welfare. Every six weeks, when he was making out his report, the teacher would ask me before the entire class, "McPherson, is your father still in jail?"

During those years at Paulson I developed a reputation for remotion. I just did not want to talk. Once, a boy named Leon Chaplin, who shared a desk with me, asked if he could sharpen my pencil with his new knife. I refused to give it to him. Leon insisted that I hand it over. I refused. He said that if I did not give him my pencil he would stab me. I refused to give it to him. Leon stabbed me, under cover of the desk, in the left thigh. I grabbed him and took the knife away. The teacher saw us wrestling and thought that I had attacked him. I told her he had stabbed me. She demanded to see the evidence. Because I would have had to take down my pants, I refused to show her the mark. After that I was watched.

During the course in first aid, we were required to demonstrate artificial respiration techniques. Our grades depended on our learned skills in this exercise. But during this time our mother was buying all our clothes from the Salvation Army, and there were holes in my shoes. For this reason, I refused to kneel down and demonstrate how much I knew about artificial respiration. I knew that the other kids would laugh at the holes in my shoes. I did not want them to laugh. The teacher kept demanding that I kneel down. I kept refusing. I finally flunked the course.

But during this same time, I discovered the Colored Branch of the Carnegie Public Library less than a block away from where we lived on East Henry Street. I liked going there to read all day.

Books

At first the words, without pictures, were a mystery. But then, suddenly, they all began to march across the page. They gave up their secret meanings, spoke of other worlds, made me know that pain was a part of other peoples' lives. After a while, I could read faster and faster and faster and faster. After a while, I no longer believed in the world in which I lived.

I loved the Colored Branch of the Carnegie Public Library.

"Daddy Slick" and "Mama Della"

These were people who had no respectability. They were my father's friends. They owned and ran a place on 32nd and Burroughs streets where men gambled and where moonshine whiskey was sold. I loved to go in there and look for my father. He loved to gamble and be in there with the other men.

To get into Daddy Slick's place, you had to walk through the dry black dirt on Burroughs Street until you came to a big yard enclosed by a high wooden fence. You could not look over the fence, but you could ring a buzzer on a wooden door in the gate. A peephole would open, and you had to say to someone, "Is my daddy here?" Once you were recognized, the wooden door would open and you would be allowed into a courtyard where ducks and geese and flamingos and chickens were strutting and scratching in the black dirt. Directly across the courtyard was the house in which Daddy Slick and Mama Della lived. To the right of the house, at a distance, was another house, a much smaller house also made of wood. It looked almost like a toyhouse and was painted bright colors. This was where people drank and gambled. To get in, you had to knock on another wood door and be inspected through another peephole. Inside that place, it was always dark. But there would be music from a bright jukebox, and light from the pinball machines, and people would be drinking. Daddy Slick or Mama Della always sat behind the counter facing the door. They always saw you before you saw them. Daddy Slick was very fat and Mama Della was very thin. Daddy Slick always wore a round, flat touring hat. People said he had a photographic memory and never forgot anything, especially the amount of money people owed him.

He sat with his legs apart so his belly would have room to spread. He or Mama Della always gave you a Coke or an orange soda or a nickel or a dime. In the wall near the counter was another door. In that room people gambled. My father was almost always in there. I always wanted to go in there, but was never allowed to. I would have to sit at the counter and wait for him to come out. Sometimes I would play one of the pinball machines. When my father came out, he would always buy something for me, no matter whether he had won or lost in the gambling room. Once, because he had promised to buy me a television for my birthday, I played hooky from school and waited all day at Daddy Slick's for him to finish gambling. He had just won a lot of money playing bolita. But when he came out, in the late afternoon, he had lost everything. He could no longer afford the down payment on the used television set we had already chosen. He tried to give me his wristwatch instead. I refused to take it.

Daddy Slick also sold bolita. Someone told me once that my father won at bolita so often that after a while no dealer in town would sell him a ticket. But he was liked by all the men who spent time at Daddy Slick's. Whenever he was in jail at Christmas or at Thanksgiving, Daddy Slick or Mama Della, or one of the men, would bring a box of groceries to our house. These people had their own code.

James Alan McPherson

Electricity
1957

I think that a certain kind of creative man finds one thing he likes to do and then does it for the rest of his life. I think that if he is really *good* at what he does, if he is really creative, he masters the basics and then begins to *play* with the conventions of the thing. My father was a master electrician.

During one of the times he came back from Reidsville, we lived on East Henry Street. He was working again for T. J. Hopkins, and was trying to be a man in all the conventional ways. He liked to cook for us, liked to drop by the house to see us whenever he passed it during work hours. He liked to fix things. One day he was repairing the light fixture above the face bowl in the bathroom. He asked me to hold one of his hands and to grip the faucet of the bathtub with my other hand. I did this. Then he licked the index finger of his free hand and stuck it up into the empty socket where the lightbulb had been. As the electricity passed through him and into me and through me and was grounded in the faucet of the bathtub, my father kept saying, "Pal, I won't hurt you. I won't hurt you." If I had let go of the faucet, both of us would have died. If I had let go of his hand, he would have died.

That day, I know now, my father was trying to regain my trust.

Black and White

Once, when a story about me was in the Savannah papers, an old white man called up my mother. He introduced himself as a former Chatham County official who had known my father through his work as an electrician. My mother said he asked, "Is this Mac's son?" Then he said, "Mac was a brilliant man. That liquor just got to him." Then he said, "Mable, I never had anything against the colored. Now both of us are old. Can I come around sometime and sit with you?"

Richard, my brother, knows more about the public side of my father than I do. He and my father worked together on a number of jobs. He told me that when they were wiring a store for a Greek on East Broad Street, my father's and my brother's skills came under the watchful eye of a redneck. He and his son were pouring concrete for the Greek. The redneck watched my brother for a while, and then said to his son, "You see there? If *you* worked as hard as that little nigger over there you'd get someplace." Richard said he turned to my father and saw him laughing. The sight of this, considering the insult, made my brother cry. Then my father said to Richard, "Look, if you get hot over something like that, you'll stay hot all your life."

Richard also told me that part of his job with my father was to take certain papers to a state agency as soon as a job was completed. He said there was a receptionist's desk in the lobby of the building to which he was required to go. This was during the time of official segregation, and the white female receptionist would always stop him at her desk and try to prevent him from going upstairs. But then the official in charge of the agency would come to the head of the stairs and say, "Is that you, little Mac? Come on up." He would sign the papers without looking at them.

The Jewish community of Savannah, which was old Sephardic, knew and respected my father for his intelligence and skill. They knew who his children were. Sometimes on Christmas Eve, when our lights were off and we had no food or presents or Christmas tree, my father, if he was not at Reidsville, would appear well after dark with money he had either borrowed or won at gambling. He would break the law by turning on our electricity himself, and then he would take us downtown to shop. Certain merchants would keep their stores open for him far past closing time on Christmas Eve. I never believed in Santa Claus, but I believed that my father, sometimes, possessed a special magic.

Last Christmas my mother gave me the best Christmas present in the world, and all Christmas Day I felt as if my father were still keeping the stores open late on Christmas Eve. She said he loved to buy groceries after he had been paid for doing a job. She said that one night he came home with sacks and sacks of groceries, bought with money he had just collected from poor white people for work completed. He told her, "Mable, those people don't have anything. They paid me because they're proud. I'm going to take half of these groceries out to them." Since my mother valued security, she said, she got very mad.

Wendell Phillips Simms

Mr. Simms ran a fish market on the corner of West Broad and Walburg streets. His father had been a slave who escaped to the North during the years just before the Civil War. He had joined the abolitionists, had taken the name Wendell Phillips, and had returned to Savannah during the Reconstruction. He brought the traditions of freemasonry into the black community of Savannah. His son, Wendell Phillips Simms, was a thirty-third degree Mason. I did not know this when I was growing up.

Mr. Simms had five children: Robert, Ruth, Merelus, Louis and Richard. Merelus and I were born on the same day, next door to each other. We were natural playmates. Mr. Simms and my father, in the early days, exchanged turns taking us to school. But after a while, they did not get along. The clash of personalities, I think, resulted from the differences in their perspectives. My father seemed to love everybody. Mr. Simms had deep suspicions of the world outside his fish market. My father drank and gambled. Mr. Simms did not. My father was always looking out for other people. Mr. Simms looked out for himself. My father took great chances. Mr. Simms always hedged his bets. My father improvised. Mr. Simms practiced great efficiency. Mr. Simms did not seem to respect my father. Whenever he spoke to me of him, I could hear condescension in his voice. Mr. Simms thought, long before I did, that my father was irresponsible.

When I went into their fish market, after school, I would talk with Merelus and Louis while they cleaned and weighed fish. Mr. Simms would recite poems like "Invictus" and "Keep A-goin'" while he cleaned fish. He knew all the nineteenth-century declamatory gestures. He seemed to believe the words he recited. He practiced great self-reliance and had a quiet contempt for Christianity. He kept his contacts with white people to a minimum. He preferred to catch his own fish in the Savannah River rather than buy them from the local wholesalers. He once attacked a truckload of Klansmen with a crowbar.

When I was about six, Mr. Simms began making bricks. He designed a device in his backyard for pressing and baking cement blocks. Over the years, day after day, he and his family made thousands of bricks. They tore down parts of their house as more room for the bricks was required. I liked to watch them from our kitchen window. Merelus and Louis and Richard would climb up the pyramid of cement blocks and talk with us through our kitchen window. My father agreed to do the wiring for the new house, and I wanted very badly for him to have some part in the creation. But by the time the house was ready for wiring he had lost control of his own life. Mr. Simms finished the house, by himself, and moved his family into it. I was invited there to visit a number of times. Mr. Simms had broken his health completing the house, but he was very proud of what he had done. When he spoke of my father, there was that familiar contempt in his voice. He died, in the house, shortly after he had settled his family into it.

Several years later, the Urban Renewal leveled the entire west side of Savannah, including Mr. Simms's house, to make room for a massive housing project named Catton Homes.

Mr. Hopkins under the Neon Light

We owed Mr. Hopkins many hundreds of dollars when we moved out of his duplex on Montgomery Street. He had offered to let us stay, and he offered to let my brother and me work for him, in the absence of our father, in order to pay off the debt. My brother, Richard, did work for him for a while, but then my mother found another apartment and insisted that we move. We moved into an apartment in a slum that had many rats. I could not understand why she had not accepted Mr. Hopkins's kindness.

Years later, when I understood, I thought that Richard should be the one to repay Mr. Hopkins the money we owed him. I wrote a check for a certain amount and gave it to Richard and asked him to go in and put the money on Mr. Hopkins's desk. I don't know whether Richard ever turned over the money. I don't know whether he ever understood.

In the Fish Market

Louis Simms is the third son of Wendell Phillips Simms. Unlike Merelus, he left Savannah. Like his oldest brother, Robert, he joined the U.S. Army and became an officer. He served in Vietnam, then in Europe, then returned to Savannah to be close to his mother. When Mrs. Simms died, he moved to Michigan to be close to his older sister, Ruth. Both he and I wound up in the Middle West, and we have a bond based on common memories. Louis remembers all the details.

Since childhood, Louis has kept everybody honest. He tells the truth, even though it hurts. Sometimes I feel that his father and my own are still debating essential issues: the advantages of efficiency over improvisation, the self-negation that can come from Christian belief, whether it is better to laugh at or to attack intruding Klansmen, whether it is best, or extremely dangerous, to call attention to intelligence and ambition in black males. Louis is wise in a pragmatic sense. He spent most of his boyhood making cement bricks.

Once, years ago, I was invited back to Savannah by the Poetry Society of Georgia. They asked me to give the Gilmer Lecture. It was a ritual occasion. The obligation of the exile is that, when he returns home, he must take something beautiful with him. At the time of the speech I had nothing to take home except forgiveness for my father. But to forgive him, I had to forgive the entire community. I wanted, twenty years late, to give a funeral oration for an intelligent and creative man. I wanted to say to the people, "This is a small part of the good thing that was destroyed." In the speech I gave I tried my very best to do this. My uncle, Thomas McPherson, was in the audience. He told me later, "James, you sure were generous to Savannah." But Savannah was also part of my father. I was trying to take the best parts of him home for burial.

Sometime later, I let Louis Simms read the speech. He called to my attention some of the concrete details that I had left out. He said:

"Although I followed the themes of your Gilmer Lecture—the merging of white and black cultures, your personal growth, the myth of racial classification, and change—I found some elements of the Savannah experience (the Southern experience, really) missing, and others, incredulous. I found it incredulous, totally unbelievable, that you could remember *no* specific incidents of oppression, to yourself or others around you. It is *impossible* for you to have been born in the South of the forties and not have experienced specific incidents of racial oppression. You may have suppressed those experiences in your subconscious, but they happened.

"You sharply forgot to mention that time and time and time again, your father had been unjustly denied an electrician's license—and he was the best. Yes, Mr. Mac was the best, or so my father and mother told me. My father and mother also told me, and my brother and sister, that the lily-white test administrators would never release your father's test results. This refusal by *white folk* to grant your father an electrician's license and release his test scores, along with scores of other rejections and humiliations—the inheritance of all black people—caused your father irrevocable pain. The pain may have even caused him to masquerade—as many unpleasantries have undoubtedly caused you to masquerade—his hostilities toward whites. He turned to drink for relief, you turn to 'ideas.'

"Those black folk who did not have other escape mechanisms, had to masquerade, or face the sure prospect of being blown to pieces, physically and psychologically. Believe me, your father's alleged status as the first black master electrician in Georgia came at a terrible drain on his inner resources. His effort to become an electrician, much less a master electrician, was a great leap from the abyss of despair. I'm not talking abstractly now. Two years ago, I did a paper for an E.E.O. case in Labor Relations on 'Blacks and the Law in Skilled Trades.' The electrical trade was, and still is, more discriminatory towards blacks than any other skilled trade. The electrical trade, in fact, has almost totally excluded blacks. When writing this paper, so as not to become abstract, I thought of your father, Mr. Mac . . ."

The Ancestral Home

There is not one house where I lived as a child still standing. My family is scattered. All of us have, in one way or another, gone up to Atlanta. But my mother still resides in Savannah. Her one ambition, for many years, was to have us all come home. We went, whenever she was sick, but we could not stay there with her.

My brother lingered in Atlanta, biding his time. He has my father's genius for things electrical and mechanical. He is a mechanic for a major airline. For years now, he has been the only black mechanic in his shop. He once expected promotion to foreman of his shop. He took the standardized tests and outscored his peers. The rule was changed to make the election of a foreman democratic. He played politics, made friends, did favors. Finally, a somewhat friendly white peer told him, "Mac, your only trouble is your father was the wrong color." After every new foreman is elected, my brother still receives calls at his home during his off hours. These calls are from his peers, and they explain technical problems that they cannot solve. They ask, "Mac, what should we do?"

My brother, Richard, is "Papasqualli" now, up in Atlanta.

Many years ago, I tried to go back as close to Savannah as I could. As usual, my mother was calling all of her children home. It was my fate, on the way back to Savannah, to enter a time-warp in Charlottesville, Virginia. I lived, as an intelligent black male, through the first fifty years of this century. And when, some years later, I emerged, I found that I had learned, emotionally, every previously hidden dimension of my father's life. I love him now for what he had to endure. I am determined now, for very personal reasons, to live well beyond the forty-eight years allotted to him, in any Atlanta I can find.

Like all permanent exiles, I have learned to be at home inside myself.

A Positive-Negative

There is, I know now, in the hidden places of human nature, a lust for power over the souls and the talents and therefore the bodies of special people. I don't believe there was any of this craving in my father. He had a passion for something that transcended it. He loved electricity, loved to play with it, and must have found some connection with God within the mysteries of that invisible flow. His will to believe in this, I think, allowed him to maintain the illusion that people were better in fact than they are in life.

For forty-eight years, I want to believe, he practiced an enigmatic form of his own secular religion.

Obligations

Honor thy father and thy mother:
that thy days may be long upon the land
which the Lord thy God giveth thee.

The Book of Exodus

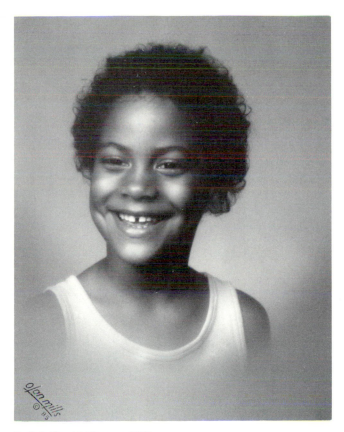

Rachel Alice McPherson. 1979– .

THE POWER

AND THE

GLORY

ROBB FORMAN DEW

I had a wonderful personality until I was about fourteen when I was simply too tired to have it anymore. Now and then, in the following years of adolescence, I made a supreme effort to draw remnants of my former sparkling self around my new and listless persona, but it was no use; I could only maintain the effort for short sprints. I had already made my long run in life. In fact, I suppose I reached the pinnacle of my success when I was in the eighth grade, and it had been an arduous and strategically planned battle all the way.

My three best friends were all named Elizabeth, and I've thought over the years that those Elizabeths probably did, unwittingly, keep me tethered at least to a half-hearted pretense of normalcy during several years when it hardly seemed worth holding on to. My eventual apathy was like a disease of the fiber and bone of the body, and, as it happens, I was in the company of the three Elizabeths, and a Sharon and a Linda—all of us thirteen in that year in which I had unknowingly reached the apex of my career—when I began to lose my understanding of how to be sweet, of how to be cute; or perhaps I really and truly lost the desire.

Baton Rouge was a rather shabby town when I was growing up, but I had no idea of that; I thought it was a splendid place. My father had set up

Westdale Junior High Homecoming Court. I am second from the right. Age 14 (1959).

practice there as a neurosurgeon in 1950, when I was four years old, and so it was my hometown, and therefore, in my mind it was the most desirable location in the world, because *I* was in it. I didn't really know then that I didn't belong there at all, that I was there on sufferance, my presence tolerated for a number of complicated reasons, not the least of which, I imagine, being that my father was the only neurosurgeon in that town of a hundred thousand or so people, each one of whom was vulnerable to head and spinal cord injuries at any given moment.

But on the afternoon of the beginning of my malaise I was still wrapped in the lovely solipsism of Southern girlhood, and I had set out with my friends entirely unaware that I was on the verge of being forced to break out of that soft cocoon, and not as a butterfly, but as some ungainly thing, unable to function well in the world, a fluttering sort of monster. In any case, it was a Saturday in the fall, and my friends and I had caught the bus to go downtown and eat lunch in the Green Room of the D. H. Holmes department

Robb Forman Dew

A photo I took of downtown Baton Rouge in 1958, from the window of my father's office. The D. H. Holmes department store, where young ladies shopped and where we went to lunch, is on the left.

store, go to a movie, and then, perhaps, we would take the ferry across the river to Port Allen and come back again before figuring out how to find the bus that would take us home.

I cannot convey to my children, who at fourteen and sixteen are already more worldly, in many ways, than I am myself, the exquisite sophistication of our plans for this day. To take the bus downtown! To have luncheon in the restaurant on the third floor where ladies stood waiting for the hostess to unhook the red velvet rope and admit them to the dining room beyond, and we, too, would be admitted. We wore stockings and low heels to match our leather handbags, and we were carefully blasé, but I don't believe it was only I who was filled with exhilaration at the notion of our fashionable singularity among the Saturday shoppers.

We were going to see a movie starring Paul Newman—perhaps *Exodus*, the movie was of no consequence, really. But Paul Newman had married Joanne Woodward who had, herself, grown up in Baton Rouge. The astounding co-incidence of it was almost more than I could bear, although I think I was rather more impressed than my friends. So near to fame, renown, celebrity! Every Friday of the preceding two years I had watched the "Jack Paar Show" and considered how enchanting I would be when I was a guest. I would be more delightful than Genevieve, the first celebrity I had ever heard of with one name. I would be more endearing than Dodie Goodman with her silky baby's voice. I had no reason at all to believe that I ever would be a guest, but believe it I did, albeit privately. I even secretly thought that I would probably be a famous singer, in spite of the fact that my whole family winced whenever I sang along to a record, and I had heard my mother say often enough that I couldn't carry a tune in a bucket.

So there we were in that afternoon, six young girls in the throes of an adventure. Whatever movie we had seen had been quite long, and it was unsettling to emerge from the dark, plush interior of the Paramount Theater into the warm, light afternoon. It was even melancholy in some odd way, and I don't go to movies anymore. I struggled enough with inventing a plausible reality; a visual fantasy not of my own making is still quite troubling to me.

No one was as interested as I in taking the ferry across the Mississippi, and no wonder, because there was nothing at all on the other side except man-made hills of sand and dirt and some sort of elaborate loading paraphernalia where tankers docked. We never got off there, of course, because we would have had to stand around in the dust for an hour and a half to wait for the ferry to come get us again.

It was I who insisted that we make the voyage; I was terribly bossy in my small sphere and not pleasant to be with if I did not get my way, and the three Elizabeths put up with me, as did Linda and Sharon. We crossed Third Street and walked along beside the parking lot of the Capitol House Hotel until the paved street gave way to the dirt path which went up over the levee—the only hill of any size in the whole city—and down again to the clearing where the pedestrian passengers waited to board, and we stood talking as the boat progressed slowly toward us across the water. We stood apart from the other small clusters of people who were only crossing the river to get to the other side. I don't like to remember how lovely and superior I imagined we were in our short, boxy suit jackets over our matching dresses. It seemed to me quite likely that we might be mistaken for sorority girls from

LSU, or at least some group of young women connected by their remarkable attractiveness.

We stood apart, kidding back and forth with a sort of mock and familiar scorn for one another, caught up as we were in an escalating and self-conscious animation. I think that, indeed, we really were extraordinarily lovely in our naiveté, although I have lost the image of my friends as they were at that age, and I haven't seen them for twenty years. But if we were not lovely in reality, then in retrospect I shall grant us that quality of beauty possessed by those who believe that whatever happens to them will be wonderful.

Standing slightly away from us to our left was a black man in white robes and sandals and a long gray beard who was trying to warn us and anyone else who would listen about the dire consequences of sin and evil. His words were hard to understand, but ghastly images and ideas would now and then flash to the surface, as his voice climbed up out of its angry gutteral muttering to the dreadful conclusion: ". . .and it will be the evil that will rot away your fingers one by one. The water will take you! The water will close over you! But it will not cleanse you!" He seemed to be urging us to repent before we got onto that ferry. He had a sheaf of pamphlets, and he held them out to us until we each took one, because even though we were self-involved, we were rarely intentionally cruel. We took his pamphlets and politely pretended not to hear what he was saying. We didn't want to embarrass him in case, by a look, we should be the ones to reveal to him his own, pitiable insanity. When the ferry shuddered to a stop and was moored and the footbridge had been lowered we paid our fare and crossed, surreptitiously dropping the pamphlets over the side where they fluttered past the cars, loading on the deck below, and slipped under the water and away toward the sea.

Now it is just here—when I look back and try to arrange it once again—it is just at this moment, when the bit of paper drifted from my hand and the man's voice mourned on eerily in the background, that I awakened to the whole world. Just in those few moments when I crossed the little wooden bridge did I see myself objectively for the first time in my life. It was shocking to me then, and it is shocking to me now. It is shocking that it didn't happen sooner; it is shocking that it happened at all. I apprehended at that precise moment the horrifying difference between myself and every other person in the world. It seems absurd to say so, but in the flicker of that instant I understood, although I did not yet know about them, all the horrors of the world, the evils of humanity, and also I perceived that which might be grand, the acts of honor and nobility. All at once, and for a moment, I knew everything, even the fact that I was never going to be on the "Jack Paar Show."

It was my first experience of what became an unnerving and recurring condition of being my own self while also being beyond the limitations of *person*, so that something of me also existed as an impartial observer. I saw the six of us there as we crossed the little boardwalk among a few other white people and a fairly large group of blacks, some of the women still in their white maid's uniforms. They were talking and laughing among themselves, too, but they were not paying us the slightest attention, as I had imagined they had been, and they were not self-conscious; they were simply going home from work. It seems impossible, now, but for the very first time I realized and understood that my friends and I and a few others were automatically drifting to one side of the boat discreetly marked "White" and that all these other people moved along to the other side marked "Colored." I don't know that it would be quite right to say that I was especially disturbed or upset about it; it was simply that I had never noticed our separateness until that instant, and it would be a long time before I grasped the whole story.

Our side of the boat held perhaps only five or six people other than ourselves, and the three Elizabeths and Sharon and Linda all talked to me and to each other as we chose our places on the most desirable benches against the outside railing. The other side of the boat was almost full, and the benches that looked out over the water were filled, so that some people stood at the rail next to their friends to continue their conversations. I was preoccupied and still struggling with this new and peculiar apartness from my own self, and suddenly in the middle of the river, about twenty minutes from shore, the ludicrous and obvious metaphor into which I had entered as a living breathing participant lowered itself upon me. "You know, this is ridiculous!" I said, although it was almost spoken only to myself; it was just a remark. "We're all on the same boat!"

My friends were startled, but it was clear to me in a second that this information was no surprise to them. They had always understood this condition, but their expressions reproved me just for the saying of it. Clearly it was not *done* to declare this obvious fact; I understood that within an instant of having spoken it aloud. It was not that those girls begrudged me this early observation, or even gave me up later when my views became more vehement. It was not, I'm afraid, even noble that, having suddenly become aware that the world contained more than my own self, I gave up being as cute as I could be. I'm ashamed to say that that afternoon on the ferry it wasn't sudden outrage at the idea of racism that struck me such a blow. What really happened on that boat, and at that particular moment, was that I was forced to begin a long process of acknowledgment of the stratifications of ambiguities upon which I had constructed my idea of success in the world.

Over the years that I had lived in Baton Rouge I had invented not just the political but the social and personal realms of my life, and all of a sudden the fragile structure of my whole existence would no longer hold steady. Over the next three or four years I was forced by the conflict of my own desires and sensibilities into an involuntary abdication of any power I had accrued.

But until that day, before my life became complicated by any real exercise of my intellect or even of my curiosity, I had managed to attain all the heights to which I aspired. In the first grade, when Mrs. Fogelman announced that we would be electing a boy and girl in two categories—"Most Popular" and "Best All Around"—I set my mind on becoming one of the two girls to win one of those titles out of my class of thirty.

My obsession with this validation of my acceptability was formidable, and it wasn't until recently that I realized that the quality of my obsession, alone, may well have compelled my classmates to elect me to one of those superlatives year after year all through grade school, and then in junior high school to other things—homecoming courts during football season, or Mardi Gras Ball courts in the spring.

As I defined life in my early teens, social victories were the only justification of my existence. There always was some proof of popularity to be contested, and my quest approached desperation, because I had already begun to understand that my family life was considered unusual, a subject of curiosity among the parents of many of my friends. I learned fairly early that my best tactic was to endorse the notion of a sort of adorable eccentricity, which took a certain flair on my part, because I was reinterpreting what must have been an encroaching claustrophobic despair closing in on my parents in the determinedly ordinary society in which they were trying to make a life for themselves.

My father had gone from Natchez High School, in the late thirties, to Ole Miss, to Vanderbilt, to Johns Hopkins, and on the way he had gone from being a political conservative—probably a discreet bigot—and a devoted Episcopalian, to being an advocate of integration and a militant atheist, full of relatively radical ideas and beliefs and what I now know was ridiculous optimism. He was a handsome man, and I really think he was convinced that

Mardi Gras Ball Court at Westdale Junior High School (1959). I am second from the right.

he could change other people's minds simply by his power of persuasion. When I was young, people used to tell me that my father could charm the birds right out of the trees, and I think it was something he believed himself.

My mother's father was the poet and critic, John Crowe Ransom, and she had lived all her life in a household where ideas were exchanged. I don't believe it ever crossed her mind not to have any. She was—and still is—a brilliant woman, eccentric in the sense that she cannot conceive of an unexamined life, nor can she pretend to live one. And I think that Baton Rouge was unique in the South of the fifties in that it was too young a society to tolerate anything it might perceive as eccentric. This was so in a broad sense; there were people who were wonderful and loyal friends to my parents. But Baton Rouge was already starting to boom; people were moving into the area from all over the country to work in the huge petrochemical industries in all sorts of capacities, and the situation was probably threatening to a relatively newly established social order. And my mother was as beautiful a young

Robb Forman Dew

woman as my father was handsome. They were an astonishingly striking couple in a region where beauty carried with it such suffocating expectations. Probably nothing could have stopped the disintegration of my family under the weight of my father's alcoholism, but it has always seemed to me that my parents were not prepared to have ordinary expectations; my father was— and my mother is—extraordinary. I think their marriage was done in partly by the simple *dailiness* of life.

Wedding picture of Helen Elizabeth Ransom and Oliver Duane Forman.

When I was growing up in the South it was expected by polite society that one be faithful to God and beauty. Luckily the idea of beauty was subject to interpretation and nuance, but religion was pretty clear-cut, and my family didn't have any. In my mother's case I don't believe it had ever been a question; her own family was not religious. My father, however, had been an acolyte and a crucifer in the Episcopal church when he was growing up, and all through college he remained devout. I don't know exactly when he gave up on religion, but he never got over his outrage at what he considered a terrible trick—even a conspiracy, perpetrated throughout his youth by so many people he admired and respected—designed to mislead him, as one would a child, into false hopefulness. I can only guess that it was the idea of the inherent condescension that infuriated him, and he absolutely refused to believe that anyone intelligent could also be religious. *All* of my best friends were religious, and I knew they were smart, too, so this was the first equivocation that I had let slide right by me unexamined, because I loved my friends, and I loved my father, too.

My mother was far more tolerant about the subject of religion, and really less interested in the whole issue than my father. She was enormously kind and polite to a fault, and she became a fascination, and I believe a real challenge, to the minister of St. James' Episcopal church. Mr. Werlein was a tall, patrician, white-haired man who had been educated at Sewanee, and he could hardly have helped but be intrigued by my mother, who was lovely and who had such exotic Southern intellectual connections. He was most anxious that we attend church, and my parents' friends and our neighbors often did take me along with them on Sunday morning. I think my parents were eager at least to assuage the concern among their acquaintances over my spiritual education.

It was enough for their friends, but it wasn't enough for Mr. Werlein, and he dropped by often in the afternoons to discuss theology with my mother, who I don't imagine ever had the heart to reveal to him her complete indifference and her lack of religious background. She didn't disillusion him of his idea that she and my father attended church now and then, when they were up in Natchez, or when they were away, and one afternoon she sat talking with him in the living room when he decided to pin her down on this point. "Well, tell me, Helen," he said, "how often do you and Duane *commune*?" My mother was nearly speechless, although since this was a minister, after all, and someone she had come to be fond of, she thought she ought not to be offended. "Why . . . well . . . of course, it depends . . . well, two or three times a week, I suppose. Well, I haven't ever kept count exactly, you see."

I don't know that they ever straightened this out between them. Mr. Werlein didn't come around so often after that, and once when he did my mother sent my five-year-old sister to the door to say that she wasn't at home. "She can't come to the door right now," my sister said, "because she's hiding in the closet."

Years after that, long after Mr. Werlein had stopped making his calls, and when my father's alcoholism had become so severe that there was no longer anything adorable about our eccentricities, my mother said to me that she wished she was religious, because then she would go to church on Sundays. I remember being so puzzled by that then, and I pointed out to her that as far as I could tell actual religion had very little to do with church attendance and that I was sure she would be welcome at any church on any given Sunday. "But if I really were religious," she said, "and had real faith, don't you see, I would have to get up and get dressed and go out to church on Sunday mornings."

My father also believed that there was a secret, or some special trick, to achieving if not a happy, at least a serene life. But he was an alcoholic, and that was a shameful thing, something that I refused even to discuss with my husband until almost five years after we were married. It is only a fact of my life today—that my father was an alcoholic—but the immediate families of alcoholics are locked into a peculiar conspiracy that they don't even speak about among themselves, and, really, my mother and sister and I may as well all have been afflicted. I think it must not be so different now; I bet there are still spouses and children mute with a sense of loyalty and also of shame, and living every day under an oppressive cloud of dread that hangs in the heavy air of the household. But at least society has changed a little. All kinds of famous and sometimes admirable people make it quite public that they suffer from some kind of substance abuse. We frequently see them on the news as they check into or out of the Betty Ford Treatment Center, seemingly hopeful, parrying brightly with reporters. But in the fifties and sixties it was a condition no one ever spoke of, although my father deteriorated so quickly that it certainly couldn't have passed unnoticed, and he died when he was only fifty. No one said a word to me, though, because alcoholism was not recognized as a disease; it was considered strictly a character flaw.

I once suggested to my father that he see a psychiatrist about his drinking. It was a fearsome thing to do, to make that suggestion, because he had often been furious at the idea that he had any problem. But I was so peculiarly lonely and terrified, because I had begun to hate him. I would lie in bed at night and wish with all my might, with every bit of my intensity, that he would die, and yet even in the moment of wishing it I would be overcome with the most terrible sorrow, because I also loved him in a way that only a man's daughter is likely to love him; at fifteen or sixteen I loved him more than I had ever loved any other person. Anyway, he wasn't angry but only scornful of my suggestion. "How could a psychiatrist possibly be any help to me at all when I'm so much smarter than any of the ones I know?" he said.

My father was becoming a violent and dangerous drunk, and I know that as his disease progressed he frightened himself. I know that he was very much afraid, for a while, of losing control of his life until he was so far gone into his addiction that all his power of rational judgment deserted him. Now and then he would go down to Mandeville and stay in a vacation house owned by a friend of his who was our pediatrician, and every time he would go off he would tell me that he was just going to drink beer, that he was going to give up hard liquor. "You know," he said, "if we were only Jewish we would have such a happy home life. I used to love to go over and visit Clifford Tillman when I was growing up in Natchez. I really liked to be in his house and stay to have dinner. His family was so close! And, of course, if I were Jewish I wouldn't drink."

As my father's alcoholism grew more severe I became less and less able to maintain the illusion of the perky Southern belle. I began to discard the trappings of my darling personality. The whole idea of it was so far from the truth, and it required so much energy that I just let all of it drift away.

And the contradictions abounding in my environment were becoming impossible to ignore, too. Racial tension had reached a peak by the early sixties, since the Baton Rouge school system had managed to remain segregated for such a long time after the decision of *Brown v. Topeka Board of Education*, and my friends were beginning to become politicized. I believe that my often uninformed but nonetheless passionate championship of civil rights had always been looked upon as an aberration of an otherwise perfectly normal girl, but by then the situation was getting serious. I could no longer tolerate racial jokes or any sort of racial slur, and I couldn't pretend anymore that I didn't hear them, so I was often in a position of confrontation.

It amazes me now that my good friends—male and female—did not really give me up, although I imagine some of their parents wished they would. While the father of one of my good friends was heading up the White Citizens' Council, my own father was meeting covertly with other doctors, black and white, to try to gain access for black surgeons to the two hospitals in the city, and if *I* was aware of all this I have no doubt that it was common knowledge. In a society like the one that existed in Baton Rouge in the early sixties—an embattled system in which, at the top, the inhabitants were really just teetering on the edge of upper-middle-class—both men were extremists. I would guess, though, that the greatest sympathy lay with the head of the White Citizens' Council. But my friends were really more loyal to me, who was challenging them on every front, than I was to them, when I just gave up the fight for beauty, for charm, for grace, and for social acceptance.

When I think about it, it seems to me that there was an abundance of truly beautiful girls in Baton Rouge, girls like movie stars, but not all of them were acceptable to a middle-class society, I suppose, and so there was a whole group of what I have come to think of as *marginal* belles. Ambition could carry a relatively pretty girl a long way, and for a Southern girl in the fifties and early sixties it was absolutely crucial to be counted among the current crop of attractive girls. How else could we attract men? If we did not learn how to be lovely, how to be charming, why should we expect to marry well or to marry at all?

Our mothers suggested to us that we read books on baseball, basketball, and especially football, so that we would be interesting to some possible boyfriend who might be on the team or who would take us to a game. We heard our mothers remark that there was nothing wittier than groups of boys or young men as they played their games and joked among themselves in their high school groups and eventually in their fraternities, and we took it on faith that this must be so even if the jokes were at our expense. I have no doubt that this was hard on boys, too; but at least they only had to earn the right to judge, whereas we had to be prepared to *be* judged through every instant of our days.

It was as clear as it could be that we were expected, literally, to *attract* one of these young men, but the curious thing was that all of this striving for beauty had absolutely nothing to do with eroticism, which *no* one's mother talked about. The perfection and maintenance of one's image was primary; good grooming was of the ultimate importance, and for years my perception of beauty—in the landscape, in music, in art—was tightly entwined with the idea of order and a carefully organized kind of tidiness. Many of us became unintentionally coy, because sex is so disruptive; not much is possible without arriving home, or at a friend's house, looking disarranged. Lately I've begun to suspect that the Southern girls who got pregnant early, and disappeared from our lives, either had no ambition at all or had easily manageable hair. The cultivation of all this beauty, and all the exhausting work of acquiring charm, was really about power; it was about recognition; it would ensure glory.

We listened to snatches of conversation among parents when we were at parties, or when we happened to be in the same house with our friends' mothers. And we discussed all these matters among ourselves. We all understood the categories of beauty: there were, of course, the girls who were "absolutely beautiful," and then there were all the many girls who were described as being, each one of them, "just as cute as she can be with a *darling* personality!" This was my category when I was still competing. These were the girls who had charm, which was, I know now, a crippling thing that entailed turning one's whole intelligence toward an effort to be pleasing to other people. The kind of charm we aimed for was counterfeit, because it had nothing to do with any one of us; we were only learning how to make someone else believe that he or she was enchanting. And it turned some of the brightest girls into incredibly manipulative and secretly angry women. I meet these people still, all the time; they are certainly not all Southern, although they are all women, and there are no other social creatures of whom I'm as wary.

Then there were the girls who were "really sweet" and the girls who were "very attractive!" Of course, that only meant that these girls were not pretty and not clever and were probably doomed to live out uneventful lives somewhere on the fringes of society.

There was one final category which was just making its way into the culture, and into which one of the Elizabeths fit, and that was: "just so *smart!*" Which meant that the girl in question was not only remarkably intelligent but that she refused to attempt cuteness even though she could probably achieve it. These girls were troubling to their mothers, who sent them to charm schools, had them take dance, and who at first became alarmed and then fell into despair. These girls were a puzzle to everyone, and it was assumed that they would probably move away somewhere and have a life entirely unconnected to Baton Rouge society. "She's so good at French!" we would say. "Don't you think she could go to New York and be a translator at the U.N.?" There was nothing we could imagine more glamorous than that.

We worked so hard at being appealing! We had bedrooms that looked like beauty parlors, with storklike hair dryers, cosmetics of every variety, fashion magazines on our bedside tables. We slept miserably with enormous, bristly rollers wound into our hair and got up at six in the morning to unwind them so that we could painstakingly backcomb and construct our pageboys, bubbles, or flips. We applied makeup base, eyeliner, mascara, lipstick, and a final dusting of loose powder which we had read would *set* our makeup for the day. This was in order for us to go to *school!* For me each day was like a premiere, and, in fact, I went to school as little as possible, because putting in an appearance required more energy than I could muster.

One morning I couldn't find my eyelash curler, and so positive was I that without curled eyelashes I would be remarkable, that I would look grotesque, that I claimed illness and did not leave the house. By the time I had reached the ninth grade at Westdale Junior High School, in 1960, I no longer felt certain of my grasp of reality. If I was elected to one thing or another I began to suspect that it was because there was something terribly wrong with me—a physical deformity or perhaps some sort of obvious mental illness—that only I could not fathom but that elicited enormous sympathy from my schoolmates. I could no longer manage all the secrets of my own life in the face of the image I tried to sustain in public.

By the time I entered Baton Rouge High School, in the tenth grade, I was beginning to divest myself even of the pretense of normalcy. Not that I could have divested myself of *pretense*—after all, who in the world would I be? I adopted a sort of halfhearted bohemian attitude, which entailed not much more than slipping into the girl's bathroom in the art building at recess and smoking a cigarette. But I also began to relinquish my place in the *nice* group at school, although the three Elizabeths stuck by me even when I dropped out of the Baton Rouge High Booster Club.

All the girls from the best families were in the Booster Club, which was, essentially, a support group for all those very nice boys on the various athletic teams. One's whole class schedule was arranged around participation in this club, because all the academic courses had to be gotten out of the way before sixth period when the teams and the Boosters practiced their separate skills. If I gave up Boosters I would virtually be assured of having to give up the company of the elite of the school in any of my classes, because their schedules would conflict with mine. But I didn't care very much by then, because I loathed the whole enterprise, which required all sixty or so girls to wear identical skirts and blouses in the school colors and march into various formations on the football field at halftime, so that from the stands a message or a picture could be discerned from our clustered bodies. The brilliant

BOOSTER OFFICERS: Marilyn Meyer, Linda Hardin, Mimi Barnum, captain; Anne Affolter, Betty Heath.

I would say how nice sweet & thoughtful you but — The HAIL with it MIKE GLISSON

MRS. DREW SHAW
Sponsor

Hup, Two, Three

Go, Hawks, Go!

The top picture shows the Westdale Junior High Boosters. I am in the third row down from the top, fifth from the right.

Robb Forman Dew

Elizabeth was one of the bass drum players for the Boosters, and during one memorable homecoming parade downtown, the leather strap, with which the giant drum was suspended from her shoulder, broke, and the drum went rolling away down the gentle incline, around curves, across streets, always just ahead of her pursuit of it, to the very end of the parade route. I was exhilarated. I loved her wit, her irreverence; I thought this was a splendid joke. But when I reached her she was near tears; this was a disaster for her, of course it was! I cared about my friends intensely, but not with much sensitivity.

When I dropped out of the Booster Club, two of the Elizabeths' mothers called me up in great consternation. They were genuinely worried that I was taking an irreversible step toward ruining my life, and I was not at all sure they were wrong, but I was turning all sorts of possibilities loose, anyway. By then the strict regimen of the Boosters—the appearances to be kept up— was more than I could manage. But those two women were concerned about me, as was my own mother, and they had telephoned because they loved me, as best they could, and the brilliant Elizabeth's mother, who did not, was merely confirmed in her disapproval of me.

The drum corps of the Baton Rouge High School Booster Club.

Of course, I left Baton Rouge finally. I had always been a tourist there, anyway, or so I had come to believe. My high school adopted a generous and inventive attitude toward my curriculum, and although I left for a while during my senior year to live with my grandparents, the Ransoms, in Ohio, I returned that summer and was allowed to graduate from Baton Rouge High School after completing a correspondence course in volleyball. My education is sketchy, but I am truly a whiz at volleyball, at least from the sidelines.

I went on to LSU, and, at last, I fell in love with a foreigner. Charles Dew *was* a Southerner, being one of the few people in the world actually to have been born in St. Petersburg, Florida. But he had gone to prep school in Virginia, on to Williams College, and finally to Johns Hopkins to study with C. Vann Woodward. He was an assistant professor of history at the university, and we got married in 1968, shortly before he left LSU to take a job at the University of Missouri in Columbia.

I couldn't do anything about what I was leaving behind in Baton Rouge. My mother was doing her best to hold on to our house, which was in the process of being repossessed. My sister, a fourth Elizabeth, was only fifteen,

The house my father bought in 1950, which was repossessed in 1965.

and right in the middle of high school with college still ahead of her, and yet my mother had no way at all to make a living. No one had ever thought she would have to.

My father was living with his second wife, no longer able to practice medicine, of course, and probably waiting to die after having suffered his third coronary. By then there was very little in his nature that was still fine. At his best he was almost maudlin, and if he had had anything at all to drink he became slyly cruel. All he had left was a kind of charm gone bad. But he wasn't filled with self-pity. Somewhere along the way he had resigned himself to the fact that the splendid life he must have envisioned for himself would never come to fruition; it was beyond his grasp.

He and his new wife didn't have any money, either, and lived pretty much from hand to mouth, redeeming soft drink bottles to buy a night's dinner. The Internal Revenue Service could not believe that any doctor could be ending his life with as little money as my father had, and while the house was being repossessed they had taken apart the inside of his car, convinced, I suppose, that he was hiding cash underneath the back seat. But my parents were naively honest. They had never had all that much money, and any that they had once had they had spent with generosity and abandon. By then I don't think my father or mother or sister wanted anything at all from me. We no longer had any idea how to sustain each other, and even in retrospect it seems to me that there was nothing more any one of us could have done for the others.

I don't believe that I have ever really felt that I was a native of any place. It has turned out to be liberating, and it has served me well, in my fiction, to be a temporary visitor within my own prose. I have made a small country of the society of my husband and my children, my mother and my sister, and my close friends. I rarely venture beyond its boundaries. But from the standpoint of my youth I would have to admit that I have not made a success of my life. It's been a long time since I was just adorable, and I'm making every effort to give up being charming when it sacrifices my peace of mind. My power and my glory are not bruited about in genteel society, and it has been the most exquisite pleasure of my life to sink into such comfortable failure.

UNRIPENED

LIGHT

AL YOUNG

"Papa," I told my grandfather that morning on our way to that distant part of his farm we called the low field, "I wanna tote me a watermelon back to the house, too."

Papa gave me one of his stern, knowing looks and said, "Skippy, you b'lieve you can handle one of them big old melons?"

"OK," I said. I was four and, for some reason, the slang term *OK* was beginning to fascinate me.

My cousins Jesse Earl and Inez were walking with us, and they were far wiser to the ways of farm life than I was because they lived full-time with Papa and Mama there in Pachuta. Situated in Clarke County in the southeastern corner of Mississippi, Pachuta was a comfortable driving distance from Ocean Springs on the coast where I felt at home with my brothers Franchot, Billy and Richard. It was rare for me to be away from them, visiting my grandparents on the farm.

"Wha'cha know, Skippy?" Inez asked.

"OK," I drawled back.

The four of us were taking our own good time stepping through the weeds and clay along the path to the low field. There were several ways of getting there, but the route we chose took us through the chickenyard, around the smokehouse under my favorite pecan tree, past the rows and rows of corn that led to one of the cow pastures. After that you walked for a long time through clusters of pine and other nut and fruit trees until you came to a clearing.

Al Young

Big brother Al—that's me in the center with my arms around my brother Franchot, who isn't sure he likes being photographed, and my brother William, who looks enthralled. It's the winter of 1944 on an uncommonly cold day in Ocean Springs, Mississippi.

It's 1942 in Ocean Springs, Mississippi. That's me (with my back turned, of course) and my brother Franchot, the marvelous pianist, fooling around in our front yard. The car in the background is my dad's, and if you walked about a mile into the foreground, you'd arrive at the Gulf of Mexico.

My maternal grandfather, Jordan Campbell, was doing all right for himself back in 1944, and he'd been doing well from the earliest years of the century. He was raising cotton, corn, sugarcane, potatoes, peanuts, hogs, cows, poultry and timber. Papa owned the vast acreage and the house that stood on it, a poor-Black, country-style, wooden structure built up on stilts. As a kid I figured the space up under the house had been provided for me and Jesse Earl and others our age to crawl around and spit on long pieces of haystraw to stick down dirt holes and catch doodlebugs.

Sweet Inez's mother, as my own family would do later, had taken that train known as the Chickenbone Special up to Detroit to seek out new opportunities. My Aunt Mae, Jesse Earl's mother, was working at the Army base down in Biloxi on the Gulf, right near Ocean Springs but, like Aunt Ethel who had blazed the trail, she too, would wend her way up North. But for then, during the warring forties and the upcoming Cold War fifties, everybody was wandering back and forth, and grandchildren were forever being farmed out for long and short spells to the old folks.

"Look out when you step round here," Cousin Inez was saying. "Look like it might be rattlesnakes crawling round. Y'all remember Mama tellin us bout Uncle John gettin bit by one someplace long in here?"

Inez was a big girl, in my eyes anyway, and I loved her long legs, long hair, luscious brown skin and big, dark, soulful eyes. She must've been twelve to my four, but age didn't matter; it was the gentle, girlish motherliness of her awkward kindness and innocence that would endear her to me for the rest of my life.

"Hmmph!" said Jesse Earl, who was only a couple of years older than me. "Naw, I don't reckon we oughten take no chances."

Jesse Earl, even then, even at six, was what they used to call a good little man. Among the grandchildren, he was Papa's favorite and, to this day, I believe the old man loved him every bit as much as he did any of his own kids. But what keeps coming back every time I think about Papa is the wrinkly-browed cheerlessness that seemed to hover around him the way gnats and moths buzzed around our kerosene lamps at night.

"Oooo," I said, "I don't wanna get bit by no rattlesnake!"

"Then just look where you goin," said Papa. "It's plenty other stuff beside rattlesnakes can mess you up while you walkin these weeds, you ain't careful."

That was Papa to a T— blunt and curt, although well-meaning and wise in his sullen way.

By the time we reached the low field, which took forever, my little legs were tired. I wanted to sit down someplace and catch back all the breath I'd lost trying to keep up with the others. It was Jesse Earl's tough, country savvy that I aspired to; that's how I wanted to be. I was a little boy craving to be looked upon as a big boy capable of holding my own and doing my share.

When Papa saw me panting and looking for someplace to plop, he bent down and, looking me right in the eye, said, "Wha'cha know, Skip?"

"OK," I told him.

"Well," he said, "this here's the low field, and them's the watermelons over yonder. What say we go look at 'em?"

We walked down the rows of melons, we barefoot kids and grand old workbooted Papa. To me the watermelons looked like magic itself as they sparkled on their bellies in the dirt, still connected to their source by vines. I didn't yet know about umbilical cords and childbirth, and yet I distinctly recall the whole feel of that warm morning vibrant with sunlight. Toeing and stepping around what looked like millions of melons—baby ones, mother ones, daddy ones, and great big grandpa and grandma ones—I began to get it. It was the first time I'd ever begun to become aware in an adult kind of way how connected up everything was to everything else.

There we stopped and fooled around for a moment, looking at ants crawl totally unfelt across our happy, callused feet. Inez and Jesse Earl stalled and stooped around for the longest while before they got Papa to cut off a melon they could carry.

When it came my turn to pick one, I fell to my knees over a round, compact, greenbacked, yellowbellied baby of a melon. Right away I saw it was the only one I could possibly carry all the way back to the house. But I pointed instead at a bigger, long-headed melon I thought looked more like the size and kind the big people were choosing.

Papa snapped open his pocketknife and said, "Why don't you try it out first before I snip it?"

Jesse Earl and Inez looked at each other and laughed.

"Dog, Skippy," Jesse Earl groaned. "How you gon tote some'n that big?"

I got up and lifted the watermelon. Deep down I knew good and well it was more than I could comfortably carry, but when I saw Papa take off his straw hat to fan his face, keeping his eyes on me all the while I was trying to prove my secret point, I decided then and there that, come what may, I was going to heft that thing from the low field and tote it the whole quarter mile—a *good* quarter mile—home.

Already I could picture myself arriving at the back door, the back steps where chickens roamed and cats and kittens hung out; where Mama was going to come rushing out of the kitchen, wiping her hands on her apron, to say, "I declare, Skippy! You mean you toted that melon all the way from down there all by yourself?"

"Yes'm," I'd say.

And Papa would tell her: "Ain't he some'n, this little boy of Mary's?"

While Inez and Jesse Earl held their melons to their chests, Papa squatted and sliced mine free from its vine, then stepped back to see what would happen.

"You gon be all right, Skippy?"

"I'm OK," I grunted, wobbling a little on my legs and arching my back to make sure the melon was balanced smack up against my belly for the long march. Papa grabbed a huge watermelon for himself and carried it under one arm, which tickled me. "We better get on back," he said. "Mama'll be waitin with dinner, and we can slice one of these for dessert."

Whatever we talked about walking back to the house swept clean past me. I was straining and struggling to keep up with everybody else. Maybe nothing was said at all. Papa wasn't the most talkative of men, even when he was feeling good. The truth, though, is that all three of us kids were concentrating with all our might on keeping those watermelons aloft.

Papa was the main one whose OK I wanted. That's because I'd been hearing so much about him from the rest of the family that to me he seemed like a monarch of some kind; a patriarch certainly. I was too young, of course, to know what a successful man he was, with all those lovely daughters and handsome sons, all of them loquacious; to say nothing of his respected standing in the community. All I remember about the walk back is how hard I had to work to keep my simple feet moving and the sun out of my eyes.

We'd got as far as inside the front gate, the place where I could feel relieved because the back porch was only a few more steps past the well, around the big black iron clothes-washing pot and the honeysuckle bushes that looked out from the side of the house onto the vast and seemingly borderless cottonfield.

OK, OK, OK, OK, OK, OK, OK kept bumping through my hard little head, spurring me along, grunt upon grunt.

And then—with Papa, Inez, and Jesse Earl staring right at me, as if at some galaxy through an oversized telescope—the weight of it all finally caught up and overwhelmed me.

"Uh-uhhh, look out!" I myself hollered. And in the same breath I came back with: "OK, OK, OK!!!" The meaning of *OK* by then had shattered, and each dinky shard and broken piece of it seemed to mean something different. I didn't understand any of them. All I knew was that it sounded OK to say OK right when I was about to fumble everything, just when the watermelon could no longer stand the tortured care and attention I'd been giving it, just when it must've been feeling its loneliest for the vine and all the other brother/sister melons it'd just been severed from back there in the low field.

The thing, I swear, just slipped and squirmed and worked its way free from my hands and, *zoop!*, went splattering to the ground. The moment it happened I could smell its cool sweetness begin to spread through the sunny air and blend with the sugary fragrance of honeysuckle. And right away the bees began buzzing around the seeded red flesh and green and white rind of it as watermelon fragments whizzed everywhichway.

"*Uh-uhhhhh!*"

Whether it was Inez or Jesse Earl who groaned that final uh-uhhh I still can't say at this bend in time, but I've never forgotten what Papa said; it was something that was going to affect me deeply for a long time to come.

"Mmmm-*mmmm*," he hummed deep down in his throat, surveying the wreckage with one hand in his overalls pocket and the other fastened around his own totable melon. I wanted to vanish on the spot and slip off to that part of the barn where they stacked hay and where it was possible, or so I thought then, to turn myself into pure straw simply by wishing.

Papa set his watermelon down and jammed both hands into the pockets of his faded blue hitch-em-ups.

I gazed up at the permanent, wet half-moon circles of dark sweat in his workshirt armpits and made a connection I wouldn't be able to take apart and understand, not even halfway, until forty more years had passed.

"You see," Papa said to the sky that morning, but in reality declaring himself to everyone and everything that lay within reach of his vibrant voice. "This boy of Mary's will never amount to the salt in his bread."

I did the only thing a four-year-old could do under the circumstances: I burst into tears.

In later years I would continue to do everything I could think of to win Papa's approval, but eventually I had to accept his being the habitual grump he was. Consider the photograph of him and Mama and my Uncle Noah, still a baby, taken by the side of the old house in Pachuta in 1909, some thirty years before I would come back to Earth, and a good thirty-five years before I dropped the watermelon not far from that same shuttered window in back of them. I love this picture, which had always been around my grandmother's rooms. Later I would learn from Mama the story that frames it so perfectly.

"That's your grandfather and me with your Uncle Noah, our firstborn," she explained.

"Mama, you're beautiful!" I told her.

"Why, thank you, son."

Well into her nineties now, Lillian Campbell lives in Detroit in one of the modest apartments that her church provides its elderly members. Arthritic, Mama is confined to a wheelchair and dependent on my Aunt Lil, her youn-

Jordan and Lillian Campbell, my maternal grandparents, posing with my Uncle Noah, their firstborn, by their farmhouse in Pachuta, Mississippi. It's 1909, thirty years too early for me to be born.

gest daughter, Aunt Mae, Uncle Noah, Uncle James and others for the special care and attention she needs. But her mind is as clear as the old mineral water springs running through the backwoods of the old Pachuta homestead.

"This was taken around the side of the house off the dining room," she said. "You remember the dining room, don't you?"

"Mama, you might not believe this, but to this very day I can tell you everything about that dining room you'd ever wanna know."

"Like what?"

"Well, like all the jars of fig and peach and apple and pear preserves and jellies and jams you had stored on that shelf against the wall across from the table. And those sheets of newspaper spread out up on the wall behind all the mason jars, I can even tell you some of the articles printed there."

"Is that a fact?"

"Sure, like the Letters to the Editor column where the Colored citizens of Laurel are writing to thank the White folks for letting them have the town park to hold their annual picnic."

"You remember all that?"

"Yep."

"That don't surprise me. From the beginnin you was kinda like a little old man. You used to like to get a hot cup of tea and get off by yourself in the kitchen corner over there where the radio was and read and listen at Arthur Godfrey."

This made me laugh; it was absolutely true.

"You got a good memory yourself, Mama. What else can you tell me about this picture?"

I watched her smile and get that wistful look—part pleasure, part pain— she used to get late in the day sometimes when I was staying with her. And, thinking back on those days of hers, it's a wonder she can still smile about any of it. My maternal grandmother, who hummed spirituals from morning to night, got up at five o'clock mornings, prayed, chopped wood, carried water, cooked, gardened, sewed, washed clothes with soap she'd made herself, ironed, cleaned, looked after kids and grandkids and chickens and cows and pigs and mules, and there's no telling what else.

"I'm seventeen years old here," she said, staring back at the photograph, piercing its surface and peering deep down into it as though it were only some soft cipher laid out in shadow-lit cryptography that she alone knew how to unscramble. "And your Uncle Noah isn't even a year yet."

"How old is Papa?"

"Mmm, let's see . . . That would have to make him forty-one or forty-two, cause I wasn't *but* sixteen when we got married—and he was forty."

"That's a pretty gown you wearing."

"Thank you, thank you. I'd just finished sewin that dress a few minutes before the photographer got there. Unh-hunh, I'd just got through hemmin it, and the second I got the last stitch done, looked up and there the man was ready to set his camera up. You know, in them days gettin a picture of any kind taken was a *real* big thing. You didn't just jump up and snap no picture the way people do nowdays, and ain't even got the patience now to wait for these instant pictures to jell."

"Mama," I said, "Papa doesn't look too happy about any of this."

She laughed. "That's cause he wasn't. I had to call him from out the field to come and get dressed up and pose for the picture. And I know you know enough about your grandpa to know how much he hated for anything or anybody to take up his time while he was busy workin. Facta business, far as he was concerned, this was all foolishness that could wait till he got through plowin. Papa couldn't wait for the man to come out from under that black cloth and start packin up so the picture-takin could be over with and he could hitch Jack and Jenny back up and go back to plowin. That's just the way he was."

"I'm glad the picture did get taken."

"I am, too, son. But, you know . . . If I had it to do all over again, ain't no way I'da married that man and put up with all that hard work and mistreatment. Papa didn't know how to relax or go easy on *nobody*. He was hard on all of us.

"See," she explained, "Your granpa would say somethin like that on accounta he and your mother didn't get along all that good. She'd done run away from home while she was still a child and married A.J. over there in Laurel and had you. She was just as hard-headed as her daddy, and all he was doin was gettin back at her through you."

"Did you love him?"

"Of course I loved him. But, lemme tell you, he was one hard man to love. I used to lay up and ask myself, 'Do I love this man?' I mean, he didn't know how to lighten up and accept nobody's love. All he knew was hard work and torment. And you gotta remember, son, that Papa was a Negro man in the state of Miz Sippy, and to get anything done you had to drive yourself and be smarter than White folks. But look like Papa never learned how to let up or ease up. The minute the photographer was done, Papa put his workclothes back on and hurried back out to the cotton fields. Bless his heart!"

"You know what? I kinda look like him."

Mama took another close look at Papa in the picture, then studied me.

"You favor your granpa a whole lot, son! Specially round the forehead and nose and cheeks. Yessir, you sure do!"

It took years for me to discover that I resembled Jordan Campbell in other ways as well. When, thanks to rebirth therapy, I fully became aware of this, it provided one of the keys I'd long been missing to unlock a few inner doors.

It was during a rebirthing session with a remarkable psychic in California—a woman who had studied in the Himalayas—that images of Papa kept cropping up, and the watermelon incident in particular. Although I, a somewhat professional rememberer, hadn't been conscious of it, the watermelon sequence had a galvanizing effect on me. Yet somehow I had managed to keep this early memory filed and forgotten in some old dark shoebox way at the back of the unlit closet section of my mind.

What I ended up having to learn to do was to forgive Papa, pure and simple, just as I've had to forgive myself for harboring that grudge all that time; years that saw me always taking on more than I could possibly handle, the way I thought the oldest of seven children was supposed to do. It was a pattern that ran through everything I undertook, and that's a story in itself; a big fat novel maybe. But now that I can see quite clearly how I've spent a good chunk of my life trying to prove to my grandfather I could carry a watermelon, I feel free at last to let go of it all. Now I'm free to remember Papa fully and to love him that way, too.

Perhaps my favorite recollection of the man is from the last days of his life; that period from the late 1940s when Mama was forever reciting that old adage that goes: "Once a man and twice a child." When he wasn't poring over the pages of the big home medical encyclopedia to read up on his health, Papa, in his eighties, would roam around the house and yard absent-mindedly. Sometimes he would giggle to himself. It seems he had never gotten over June 22, 1938, the night Joe Louis got to be Heavyweight Champion of the World by knocking out Germany's Max Schmelling in the first round of their return match. Often I'd hear Papa muttering gleefully under his breath: "Joe Louis beat Max Smellin! Yessir, old Joe up and whipped that

Nazi!" Over a decade after it'd happened, the Brown Bomber's victory was still tickling Papa.

It tickles me even now to still be here to write a little bit about him, and to have on hand this classic photo of yet another moment illumined by the morning light of all pasts, all presents and all futures that will be forever flowing into the only time there ever is: the eternal now, which neither needs nor asks to be OK'd by anyone.

WHEN WE USED TO GO WHERE WE WENT

T. R. PEARSON

*I*t was hers in the first place and she let us have it, Miss Edith did, for two weeks every July on account of she didn't ever go much anyway, or mostly went farther than just there, and on account of Gonny too that was a practical nurse and stayed nights with Miss Edith who was not frail or ailing but just alone primarily and in that house of hers that a dozen people could have roamed loose in and hardly ever run up on each other at all. Her daddy had owned the cotton mill and had made a considerable fortune from it that she'd got her piece of and lived on like people don't generally get to live which meant a maid for the upstairs separate from the maid for the downstairs and a cook different from the both of them and an actual chauffeur that was truly named James and wore black chauffeur's pants with stripes down the legs and a black chauffeur's jacket with offset buttons and a black chauffeur's hat as well sometimes, a black chauffeur's hat with a shiny bill that he put on when he figured couldn't anybody he knew see what it was he had his head stuck in exactly. And she went places too, places all over that she brought back picture postcards from to show to me and my sister and my momma and daddy and Gonny also who always got

T. R. Pearson

Me and my sister and my momma and Gonny and Grandpa.

invited to go wherever Miss Edith was off to but rarely did in fact go herself
but for weekends every now and again at the Waldorf-Astoria Hotel in New
York City that they rode to in Miss Edith's Cadillac with Gonny and Miss
Edith in the backseat and up front behind the wheel James himself turned
loose and hatless on the interstate.

So she let us have it every July, let us have the house at Kitty Hawk which
she hardly ever went to likely on account of it was so very close to where she
was already as to not seem like traveling to arrive at. But we were pleased to
go there and even Grandpa went with us notwithstanding how he evermore
announced that he could not go, insisted that he could not possibly afford to
be away, that he had things to do, items to attend to.

"What things, John?" Gonny always wanted to know.

And Grandpa would breathe at her that way he could breathe sometimes that was fairly much like talking only vaguer and more deniable afterwhich he would take hold of his belt and hike his pants by it.

"Just what things exactly?"

And Grandpa would say, "Well," and Grandpa would say, "Ethel," and then would breathe again before adding to the both of them, "I've got the farm to tend to."

And Gonny would tell him back just plain, "John," and press her lips firm together.

He did in fact have a farm, did in fact own himself the very eighty acres he'd been born and raised on but didn't live on anymore and hadn't lived on since he was fifteen when he ran off to barber college in Atlanta, and when he came back an actual barber and set up shop in Reidsville down by the depot he took what parcel of the farm had been left to him and commenced to collect and buy up what parcels had got left to everybody otherwise until he had the whole thing himself, the entire eighty acres with the homeplace there in the middle of it and the pond back of that with pastures roundabout it and cultivated fields to the north and to the east too near about clean out to the highway. But he didn't tend it, didn't tend it like most people mean tend when they say that and say farm too. He let out acreage for tobacco and for corn and gave over a plot to Mr. McBride from up the road who grew melons on it mostly that we generally pilfered at least some of until my momma got caught at it by Mr. McBride himself that she dropped her hid melon in front of and the two of them together watched it roll across the ground.

Grandpa did not grow anything much but sometimes a batch of zinnias in the box beside the homeplace which was not but a cabin with clapboards over the logs and there was one room in the bottom and one room in the top and a kitchen added onto the back and a screen porch behind that and a bathroom off it, a tubless bathroom with just a toilet and a sink and a towel rack and a tissue spindle and a jug of antifreeze generally, so there was not much house to tend to truly but he did keep cows every now and again in the pastures roundabout it, so when Grandpa did say tend and did say farm together it was most usually cows he meant, beef cows which he kept about two dozen of from year to year that Grandpa would evermore call twenty-odd head in a low grave voice like he was addressing the Congress. He fancied himself a cattleman and worried inordinately about hoof-and-mouth disease because he'd heard of hoof-and-mouth disease and pink eye because he'd heard of pink eye too, and him and Mr. McBride shared the duties of seeing after Grandpa's twenty-odd head with Mr. McBride undertaking most all the serious seeing after and Grandpa doing what was left that primarily meant standing at the fence with his arms on the top wire between barbs from where he would holler across the field to his cows that way country people tend to holler which is in words sort of but not ever words entirely, and they would come to him, would cross the entire field to get at him on account of he gave them winesaps and carrots and celery tops and sometimes naked sticks of Wrigley's Spearmint gum that his cows had developed a yen for.

So he figured he was crucial somehow but never could quite persuade Gonny who figured he wasn't and just said John at him and pressed her lips firm together until he had to figure he wasn't as well, and consequently he always went once he'd gone to the trouble of insisting that he could not possibly go. It was him, then, and Gonny and me and my sister and my momma and my daddy and oftentimes my Great-aunt Bessie on Gonny's side and Tillie Gonny's colored woman too who helped to cook and helped to clean and helped mostly to keep me and my sister out of the ocean when we weren't supposed to be in it. We always took two cars, took Gonny's Buick and my daddy's white and pink Ford Esquire station wagon that hadn't started out white and pink but had simply got changed and transformed by just regular sunlight. My momma drove the Ford and my daddy drove the Buick and everybody else got divided up and segregated, and Gonny usually went with Momma, and my sister usually went with Gonny and Momma, and my Great-aunt Bessie always went with Gonny and Momma and my sister exclusively on account of Grandpa never did which Daddy explained to me was the entire point since Grandpa and Aunt Bessie plainly did not and could not possibly mix and so were made to travel on the same route to the same place but not ever at the same time exactly.

We always intended to leave early in the dark and generally did in fact get up in the dark and ate breakfast in the dark, not ever one of your light breakfasts suited for a seven-hour car ride but always one of Gonny's regular breakfasts with everything fried but the coffee and it cooked fairly strenuously itself, and mostly we even carried out the suitcases in the dark and the boxes and the paper sacks and the icechests that Daddy put the bulk of in the back of the Ford and strapped the rest of to the rack atop it while Grandpa supervised and instructed and suggested and commented and employed his hands primarily in the hiking of his trousers. Somehow, though, we never managed to set off in the dark like we always planned and meant to since aside from the getting up and the eating and the hauling and the loading there was the general securing of the house to see to which meant Daddy latched the windows and Grandpa wondered had he and Daddy unplugged the toaster and the wallclock and Grandpa wondered how come and Daddy checked the dials and the burner eyes on the stovetop that Grandpa said he'd done already along with the doorlocks that Daddy figured he'd just see to as long as he was in the house, and then Grandpa would get disgusted and spit in the toilet and flush it and him and Daddy would stand together in the back hall waiting for the tank to refill and the water to cut off. Meanwhile, the rest of us sat outside in the Buick and the Ford and supposed probably we didn't have to go to the bathroom like maybe we figured we might.

Momma followed Daddy on account of Grandpa had the state map with the picture of Governor Moore on it who'd been folded direct across the face and Grandpa evermore opened the thing before we'd got up speed good and took off his eyeglasses and pressed his nose direct up to the paper like he had to to see the towns and the highways and the tiny little mileage numbers that Grandpa felt obliged to announce from time to time, and usually when we'd set out he'd warm up with one, would say to Daddy, "Elwood, I'm showing twenty-two miles to Yanceyville."

"Right, chief," Daddy would tell him. "Twenty-two miles."

And Grandpa would draw the state across his nose in an easterly direction and then show me with his finger how we intended to get where we were going prior to handing the map to me in the backseat where I would shut it and crease it and fold Governor Moore direct across the face and then hand it back up to Grandpa who would by then be telling Daddy how Yanceyville had not ever seemed to him twewty-two miles distant. He figured nineteen at the outside, and Daddy always told him back how they'd check it on the odometer but somehow they never recollected to.

Most times we stopped first at the Sunoco station just shy of Roxboro which itself was not altogether very far past Yanceyville and so was not any considerable ways from where we'd set out from in the first place but we stopped there anyhow on account of what bumping and bouncing and such can do to a bladder especially in the early morning, and Grandpa would step out of the Buick to stretch himself and would look back to the western sky and wonder just out into the air if his cows were maybe getting rained on or about to maybe get rained on and he would indicate what clouds he could see and say how they had rain in them, how they were purely full of water, and Aunt Bessie would step out of the Ford to stretch herself and look off to the west and would say just out into the air how she did not see any clouds anywhere with any water in them that Grandpa would say a thing back to that Bessie herself would talk after that Grandpa would say a thing back to again.

Tillie let me lay my head in her lap and I slept even sometimes but mostly just listened to her and Daddy and Grandpa talk about things, grown-up things primarily that I didn't know about or care about either and people I'd never heard of too, and Grandpa said how most things were going to ruination on account of Republicans and Daddy guessed at least some of what was going to ruination was going there on account of Republicans and Tillie did not have an opinion much on Republicans because she worked for some most Wednesdays and they seemed fairly much like everybody else, and then I'd raise up and want to know where we were exactly and Grandpa would uncrease Governor Moore's face and find out as near as he could and he'd tell us how far we were from where we'd just been lately and how far we were from where we'd get to next and then he'd hand the unfolded map over the seatback and tell me, "Here."

We always stopped for lunch at a colored church outside Parmele, a colored Baptist church that was white-framed with twin steeples and tall square windows and a sizeable churchyard with cedar trees in it and white pines and yellow pines too, and those of us that were called to go deep into the trees did it straightaway while Gonny and Momma and Tillie mostly unpacked lunch from the icechests and the paper sacks and spread what they could fit onto the tailgate of the Ford and spread what they couldn't onto the roof of the Buick and usually left as much one place as the other. We had ham biscuits off a cakeplate and deviled eggs off a deviled egg plate and fried chicken off a regular dinnerplate and pimento cheese sandwiches out from a Tupperware box and potato salad like Gonny made it with considerable mustard and we had green beans too that did not my sister and me ever eat any of and sweetened iced tea out of Dixie cups, sweetened iced tea over rock ice that we all sucked on and spat and sucked on again like we wouldn't ever at the table. We finished up with pound cake and custard pie and we all went ahead and said how we couldn't possibly eat any before we ate both afterwhich there was appreciable lolling around and some fairly significant exhaling on most everybody's part followed by the general packing up that Gonny and Momma oversaw and the rest of us got in the way of but for Grandpa

Grandpa in the churchyard by the pink station wagon.

Me and my sister in the icechest.

and but for Aunt Bessie who usually had found each other by then and were caught up debating over whatever might be handy which was the local bushes sometimes that they always called different things and politics sometimes that they were evermore contentious about and people more likely than not, people that Bessie told Grandpa he knew when he didn't or Grandpa told Bessie she knew when she never had, and once Daddy had parted the factions we got away from there and on down the road, usually at least so far as Williamstown where we most times stopped at the Burger Chef on account of what bumping and bouncing and such can do to a bladder.

Things looked different the farther east we went. The land got flat and the dirt got loose and black and trees got fairly scarce and stunted. Didn't the farmers seem to cultivate tobacco much but just soybeans and peanuts mostly in fields that stretched from either side of the highway pure out of sight and sometimes there'd be a house in one, a frame house up on blocks with dogs beneath it and junk on the porch and I'd tell Tillie and Daddy and Grandpa how I wouldn't want to live in such a place and they'd tell me back how they wouldn't want to either and Grandpa would say how I'd be surprised at the way some people live, how I just couldn't hardly imagine it which some way or another led to Republicans most times that I couldn't begin to decipher the reasons for and so listened at Grandpa say what he said as I looked out my window in the beanfields and at the shacks every now and again and at the hounds roundabout them sprawled in the dirt or up on their haunches to dig at fleas and I wondered what in the world I would do if Daddy stopped the car and put me out.

The black dirt and the cultivated fields eventually gave way and things got swampy and rank for a spell after Scuppernong and on through Columbia towards the Alligator River. The trees were mostly cypress and grew in the muck and the water along the roadside and Grandpa would tell how they wouldn't rot not ever and sometimes Tillie said she saw a snake dangling and Grandpa would say back how it was a vine likely, would say back how it was not the time of day for snakes to be dangling much which Tillie did not ever contend with as she hadn't wanted to see a snake dangling or otherwise, and then we were out on the bridge over the river in the bald sunlight and could see boats rocking on the choppy water and some of them were pleasure boats and some of them were shrimpers and some of them were other things that could not any of us name. The bridge was miles long and did not any of us but Grandpa know how they'd built it and he would tell us about the rock and the concrete and the pylons and the span itself even after we'd left the thing and had passed on through East Lake and Mann's Harbor and had set out across the other one, the one over the sound that had been built with rock and concrete and pylons too and was even more miles long than the first one and finished at Manteo where I commenced to look for the ocean and most times saw it before anybody else ever had since nobody else much was looking to see it like I was.

We went north up the coast on 158 between the ocean and the sound and I would identify for the benefit of everyone else various items that struck me as worth identifying, would say, "There's the pier," and point at the pier, would say, "There's Jockey's Ridge," and point at the dune, would say, "There's that thing," and point at the Wright Brothers' Memorial all stark and upright on its hilltop, and we'd drive through Kitty Hawk and by Wink's that sold cedar boxes for the bathroom with corncobs glued inside them and that manner of item and I'd point at it too and set to looking for the house that was up the road a ways beyond it. They'd named it the Pink Perfection and it was long and was low but hardly troublesome to spy out on account of it was pink too, lively pink and in a spot where was not anything else remotely pink at all. So we'd see it long before we ever arrived at it and would ease into the driveway and flush up to the garage door so as to leave Momma room to ease in behind and then we'd all be out and headed for the ocean that we'd stand amongst the sea oats and just look at for a time and Aunt Bessie would say how it looked rough to her, how it looked considerably stirred up and Grandpa would tell her back how it wasn't hardly rough or stirred up either, how he'd seen it appreciably worse and plenty often that Aunt Bessie most usually humphed at and then departed with Momma and with Gonny and with Tillie for the house so as to leave Grandpa to look at the sky and wonder about the weather elsewhere fairly much by himself.

Miss Edith's Pink Perfection was about a third as big as her regular house and so was not but twice as big as our regular houses. There was a wing of it devoted exclusively to bedrooms and we each got one with some left over just to loiter and lounge in and track grit through when the mood struck us and there was always somewhere a vacant toilet to sit on if some one of us found ourselves of a sudden hard pressed to sit on one and usually a bathtub to soak in as well that we all did considerable of once we'd stayed out on the beach too long that we all did considerable of too. The bedroom wing gave way to a main room in the middle of the house and it was paneled round-

The Pink Perfection.

about in knotty pine which was in turn fairly completely covered over with photographs of people we could not well identify and photographs of places we had not ever been and one stuffed fish as well that Grandpa insisted was a barracuda and that Aunt Bessie insisted wasn't. We dined off the kitchen at the round table under a brass lamp, or anyhow all of us dined there but for Tillie that chose instead to take her meals at the little formica-topped table in the kitchen itself on account of that was the school she was from and so she could not manage to do otherwise. A breezeway off the kitchen connected it with the garage, a breezeway with just louvered glass for walls, louvered glass that the wind did not ever seem to let loose of and so the glass shook and rattled and made a fuss all the time which was mostly how come Tillie did not sleep in the bedroom over the garage where the breezeway gave out since she did not much want to hear the shaking and the rattling and the general fuss especially once the rest of us were asleep elsewhere.

The yard had grass in the front of it though not ordinary grass but short stiff tangly grass instead that felt like shredded wheat underfoot and prickly bushes too up next to the foundation with long pointy leaves on them and a kind of a tree down at the road that did not ever seem to have leaves on it or buds on it or blossoms on it or fruit on it and did not any of us claim to know what it was but for Grandpa who insisted it was a catalpa tree though Aunt Bessie insisted it wasn't. Didn't any grass grow in the sideyards or in the backyard either because of how the sand washed and blew but just sea oats instead that had spread down off the dunes to take hold and fairly much kept the backyard from becoming the sideyards and kept the sideyards from becoming the frontyard, and perched atop the dune back of the house in amongst the sea oats was the platform with the benches and pitched roof where we sat and watched the ocean together and by turns, early and late, so that did not the bench go unoccupied but in the plain middle of the night and sometimes not then even.

So once we'd looked at the waves and once we'd poked roundabout inside the house and once we'd gone back outside to empty the cars the most of us generally sat for a time in the main room and gazed out through the glass doors at what little piece of water we could see and Daddy would say to Grandpa, "Well, here we are, chief," and Grandpa would tell Daddy back, "Yes sir," and it would seem to me just then, just that very moment, that two whole weeks was surely the kind of thing that could go on forever without getting spent and without getting used up at all.

We didn't but usually do most of the same things we'd done the year previous at Kitty Hawk which were themselves regularly the things we'd done the year before that which was partly on account of our choices were not altogether considerable and which was also, whether we knew it or not, partly on account of did not we want to do but what we'd done previously just like we'd done it so as to demonstrate for our own satisfaction that one piece of our lives did in fact hold steady while everything else refused to. Consequently, we always set out with a swim straightoff, me and my sister Bev and Daddy and Grandpa that waded mostly but went anyhow and watched the rest of us go up to our armpits in the most extraordinarily cold water I have ever got wet with, the sort of water that has never been even remotely acquainted with the Gulf Stream, so we shrieked and shivered and walked across the sandy bottom all stiff and goosepimply and could not bend our legs much and could not wholly raise our arms or wholly lower them either until after a time when we simply went dead everywhere the ocean covered.

Gonny always cooked shrimp the first night from the market up the road and as her and Momma and Bessie and Tillie shelled and veined it they generally told each other how they hadn't seen such shrimp not ever and held up for viewing specimens to verify as much, and Gonny boiled the little ones and dredged and fried the big ones and made cole slaw with vinegar in it and hushpuppies with sugar in them and served what potato salad had survived lunch and we sat at the round table under the hanging light but for Tillie that sat in the kitchen like she insisted on and talked at us through the door like we talked at her back, and when we were done we still did not get up but just pushed the dishes aside and sat for a while longer speaking at each other and listening at each other and yielding at last to Grandpa and to Aunt Bessie too who could not seem to give out of talk in each other's company and simply grew increasingly contrary until they were both far too offended to speak.

Mostly after supper we just loitered, loitered outside some in the seabreeze and loitered inside in the main room where me and my sister stretched out on the oval rug and she drew pictures on account of she could and I read funny books on account of I couldn't and Grandpa wondered about the weather elsewhere and Momma and Gonny and Aunt Bessie talked about some people that were dead and some people that weren't, not anyhow that they knew of, and Daddy threw in sometimes but mostly read what magazines he could discover which would be usually the same magazines he had discovered the year before and that he would interrupt himself in the midst of so as to tune Miss Edith's black tabletop radio that we picked up Cuba on. We played Scrabble at the supper table when someone bothered to say how we might ought to or Chinese checkers or Parcheesi and canasta every now and again that Gonny had taught me and my sister the rules of, and Grandpa that did not care for Scrabble or Chinese checkers or Parcheesi or canasta either most times fell asleep upright on the sofa and snorted himself awake at intervals while we tried to be quiet but weren't and Momma generally made popcorn in a saucepan and me and my sister got to split a Sundrop and we ate and drank and forgot whose turn it had come to be and listened to exotic music and static and Spanish voices on the radio.

Mornings mostly we walked on the beach before breakfast and picked up shells and hunted for sand dollars and poked jellyfish and found pieces of things we could not well identify and looked out over the ocean with Grandpa's binoculars hoping to see a fish jump or something better even like Momma and Tillie had seen something better that one time, had seen an actual wood chest bobbing on the water and had watched it drift shoreward

When We Used to Go Where We Went

Tillie looking out to sea.

My daddy and my sister on the beach.

as they'd decided who'd get what part of the riches inside and how come, and Tillie said it was all hers on account of she'd seen it first and Momma said it wasn't on account of she'd seen it too, but Momma was the one that hauled it in from the surf and looked inside it straightoff and saw that it was garbage from a boat and so said it was in fact all Tillie's who looked in the thing herself and decided she'd rather it wasn't.

After breakfast we generally got sunburned since we didn't figure we could, or anyhow me and Momma and Daddy and Bev got sunburned on our shoulders and down our backs and on the tops of our feet while Grandpa that wore a hat and shoes and shorts with a pajama top tucked into them most times just had his shins turn a little red on him and Gonny and Aunt Bessie and Tillie stayed places the sun couldn't reach except when they felt bold every now and again which was Gonny and Aunt Bessie almost exclusively and not Tillie hardly ever, and would sit down in the water in their regular housedresses as they did not own swimsuits any longer like they had once.

Aunt Bessie and Gonny and Bev in the cold water.

Gonny always cooked a dinner though everybody told her she shouldn't on account of she was on a vacation which did not seem to her reason enough to leave her people to eat cold food in the middle of the day, so she always cooked a dinner and the most of us slept after it on account of we were on a vacation too, and once we'd woke up and revived we generally wondered what we ought to do and determined to swim most times as we could not ever seem to recollect how cold the water had been the day previous until we got back into it the day after. But every now and again we determined to do something elsewise instead, decided to ride in the car down to Wink's and look at the lacquered shells and the cedar boxes and the tiny outhouse that squirted water when you opened the door to it or figured we'd stop in at the Wright Brothers' Memorial and see where the plane left from and where the plane landed and listen to the taped speech at Orville

Navy blimp at the Wright Brothers' Memorial.

and Wilbur's workshop like we listened to the taped speech every year or guessed maybe we'd ride all the way to Hatteras, supposed we'd take the ferry over the inlet and drive to the lighthouse and climb to the top of it so as to look off and get gnawed on and tormented by green-headed flies and mosquitoes like we always got gnawed on and tormented at Hatteras though we did not ever seem to remember from year to year how purely intolerable it all was until we got reminded, and sometimes just Daddy and just Grandpa went off in the Buick themselves and drove the coastline up through Anderson and Duck and to the end of the road at Corolla where they stopped and talked to what people would talk to them back and they even went into Virginia when they felt the urge to, in fact went into Virginia once with Gonny's dinner roll dough that she had set in the back window of the Buick to rise and had not anticipated it would fairly completely tour the countryside like it did.

Of course we fished too, felt obliged to fish as we'd carried with us our rods and our reels and our ocean tackle and on the way had spoke of how we would fish and had spoke of what we would catch and how we might in fact even eat it fresh and straightaway and not later and frozen like most times before. We baited with shrimp on a double rig, or anyhow that's what we called it as double rig sounded apt and nautical, and since I didn't have but a little Zebco on a short rod my tackle bent and taxed the thing so that it always looked to me like I'd hooked a dinghy when mostly I hadn't got even a sniff from anything. In the mornings we fished the surf because Grandpa said the surf was where the fish would be in the mornings for reasons Grandpa could not ever fully illuminate and explain once Daddy had pressed him to attempt it like he tended to, and we waded out and cast and reeled and moved up and down the beach where we figured fish might be but usually weren't, and we did not ever catch anything hardly but for Daddy who had a talent for crabs that would hold to his line long enough to get yanked from the water and airborne and but for Daddy and Grandpa together one time who came upon a pair of sandsharks trapped by the tide and dispatched them with a piece of plank.

We generally tried the pier late in the day or at night and with about as much luck as the surf brought us, or me and Daddy and Grandpa anyway fished with what luck we'd fished with earlier while my sister actually succeeded better, actually caught things and with considerable regularity on account of she had the disposition to squat somewhere and stay squatted and

Sandshark and Grandpa.

T. R. Pearson

My sister in her fishing squat.

the rest of us didn't, the rest of us had to move up the pier and down the pier and back up the pier again and just paused where she was long enough to take off her line what she had hooked that was regular eating fish sometimes but that was a blowfish once and a skate once too, and the only thing I ever caught to rival her was the flounder that I didn't even know I had until somebody else told me I had it and people gathered roundabout me to look at it once Grandpa had got it to the decking and they said it was a fine and beautiful fish and Grandpa said it was a fine and beautiful fish himself as he reached for the hook and got bit by my flounder that laid Grandpa's finger-end open.

But mostly we didn't do anything in particular, mostly we just wandered along the shore and up onto the dunes and into the water and back out again and used Grandpa's binoculars to try to spy what people we could spy on the beach which was not ever any hardly as the emptiness roundabout was purely extraordinary and complete that surely me and likely my sister did not full well notice until later when we'd been places otherwise where we could not come to be alone no matter how we attempted it. And when

My sister Bev and Tillie.

Gonny grew irate with Grandpa and with Aunt Bessie and with the general friction between them she would send them out to us on the beach and I would scoop out a hole for Grandpa and my sister would scoop out a hole for Aunt Bessie and they would sit and let us cover over their legs with the warm sand that they both agreed eased and soothed their joints considerably though they differed as to how. We'd look at boats with them, boats out on the horizon that we couldn't see but pieces of, and would look at the gulls and the seabirds and would show them things we'd picked up and kept and Aunt Bessie would speak to Grandpa of somebody she insisted he knew that he'd say he never heard tell of and then we'd watch the big silver blimp from the Navy yard drift north up the coastline towards the base in Elizabeth City like it did every evening along about suppertime and Aunt Bessie would want to know what it was made from anyway and Grandpa would tell her what it was made from precisely that Aunt Bessie would assure him it wasn't.

So we swam in the frigid water and wandered the beach and rode up to the store and back and down the other way too sometimes just to see what was down there and we laid on the dunes amongst the sea oats and listened to the wind blow through them and sat at the round table and talked to Tillie through the kitchen door and listened to Cuba on the radio at night and sometimes went out all together onto the beach where we laid our heads back and looked at the sky that there was so considerably much of with the ocean on one side and the sound on the other, and Grandpa would point out what constellations he knew which was the two dippers mostly and would raise up his arm and indicate with his finger a spot of light he would insist was Mars and Aunt Bessie would look up along his arm and along his finger and say how it wasn't Mars at all, how it wasn't but a star way off somewhere and she would raise her own arm and point off another way entirely. "Mars" she would say that Grandpa would humph at and then would not anybody but breathe and but look and but wonder too.

Then it would all be done and over with and we would commence to think about leaving for home and would commence to talk about leaving for home and would in fact pack up what we had brought that never seemed to fit quite in what we had brought it in like it had fit when we had brought it. We left early in the day to go home like we had left early in the day to come, and we'd ease out the drive and ease up the road so us in the Buick and them in the Ford could look at Miss Edith's pink house that we would not see again until the next summer brought us back. And we never figured we wouldn't go back until the year we didn't go back anymore that was the year Gonny had her operation that she never got better from. We went to the mountains instead with Grandpa and didn't ever need to speak of why to know why exactly. But even Grandpa is gone now and Aunt Bessie is gone now with him, so we could likely go back, me and my sister and Daddy and Momma and Tillie, because they've all been gone for such a long while that maybe we would find it only a little sad to be where we'd been and recollect what we'd done there, but we won't in fact go back, won't ever go back anymore on account of now we're all older and now we're all different and now we're all the same too, the same mostly.

Me pondering.

YOUR OWN

BEAUTIFUL

LIE

BARRY HANNAH

"Second Lieutenant Thomas Rivers King, Jr., of Leland, son of Mr. and Mrs. T. R. King of that city, received his wings and commission on graduation from the Army Air Corps Flying School at Valdosta, Georgia." The local paper had it something like that when "Bootsy"— my uncle, brother of my mother—got the fatal privilege of flying against Rommel when we were hitting the Nazis in Africa. Bootsy was handsome and strong, a bit over six feet, looking a little mean in the photo but with his smile he was close in looks to the old movie star Buster Crabbe. Bootsy was the ghost of my home in Clinton, Mississippi.

He was piloting his B-24 when it disappeared over the Amazon jungles en route to bomb Erwin. His history is like an old movie cut exactly in half. In Forest, Mississippi, he wrestled a bear to the ground and the bear's handler wouldn't let him try for the five dollars again. When he died or disappeared—the family never, till this day, has known what happened to him or his plane—he was just twenty-three years old. Just nine months before his disappearance he had married a luscious beauty named Hazeline. He had courted her at Mississippi Southern, where he was a football hero, despite the fact he had never played the game until he set foot on the turf in Hattiesburg.

Receives Wings

LIEUT. T. R. KING, Jr.

LELAND FLIER COMMISSIONED

Second Lieutenant T. R. King, jr., of Leland, son of Mr. and Mrs. T. R. King of that city, received his wings and commission on graduation from the Army Air Corps Flying School at Valdosta, Georgia.

He arrived during the Christmas holidays and visited relatives and friends in Leland and Greenville.

Bootsy, they tell me, laughed all the time, just laughed about nearly everything. His spirit enchanted me throughout all my youth, and remains with me whether there's a photo to look at or not. When he left us, I was too young to do any of the mourning, but somehow I remember how my mother wept, even though I was almost zero years of age. She had cherished her baby brother so terribly much, through his babyhood and childhood. Once —Mother told me—there was a big storm in the Delta where her father was a plantation manager, and the wind blew in a window directly over the bed where Bootsy was sleeping. The sisters, other brother, and grandparents rushed into the room, knowing the little lad was sliced to bits. Shattered glass was all around him and all over him. He hadn't suffered a nick.

My young mind was filled with airplanes and the men who flew airplanes. I was eventually in the Civil Air Patrol, which had its pathetic little meetings in some old converted hangar, as I recall, near Hawkins Field in Jackson, the state capital eight miles east of Clinton. These affairs were so disorganized I don't even remember who the honcho was. Some girls drank beer out in their cars, and I guess they were sort of young air whores, but God knows, at that time I was barely ready for a cigarette, me and Ray Wiley, Wyatt Newman, maybe Frank Hood, all of us from Clinton junior and high school. Some adventuresome girl named Betty Belcher was around but everything else except her name is a goner in my memory. Wait: maybe she *smoked*. A Salem cigarette was still a pretty illicit trip around Clinton—very Baptist—in the late fifties. May the gods of the air protect Betty's and my lungs, if she's still puffing; certainly, please, mine, as I suck the old Marlboros at the typewriter right now. I tell you, even the deck of my Smith-Corona puts me in mind of the panel on a jet.

The bird we were all clambering to get aboard was the Piper Cub, a silver one. First we learned to fly (or sit right), then we were on constant alert for corpses, or flood victims, fires, lost woodsmen and their families, criminals, and other direments in the thick vegetation of Hinds, Madison, Rankin, and Warren counties.

But my dream was that a brave or errant Mig-17 would whip by and you could blow it out of the air with the sawed-off .410 shotgun you'd managed to smuggle on board. We learned the use of binoculars, but secondary was some stranded couple on a sandbar in the Mississippi River. I wanted to spot a grinning gook in his cockpit in the air right beside me, then use the binoculars to see his expression after the birdshot had visited his face. Then perhaps watch the smoking trail of his doomed jet going down into the swamps of the Pearl.

I still like leather pilot's jackets. Have had several. Still love the cigarettes. I don't even hunt, but like a child I like to see what my pump .410 does to a flying beercan.

Four years ago I was visiting with some pilots down at Miramar Naval Air

Base, San Diego. The ones I was with, along with an actual heroic pilot friend of mine, from my old neighborhood, John Quisenberry, were fine guys, but I missed the old leather jackets. At thirty-nine years of age, knowing all about modern F-14s and the like, I was yet hurt a little that they were just sitting there, drinking tea and slight beer, in boring tan shortsleeve outfits, looking just a little more menacing than clerks at WalMart's, where I buy my ammo here in Oxford. America was at peace, these were reserve flyers on their monthly tests, but still I was hurt. I was having more adventures on Quisenberry's Triumph motorcycle getting back and forth from San Pedro to Bob Altman's Studio in Santa Monica than *they* were, it appeared to me. Bootsy was with me, and I wanted him to be with them. When I was in Grand Forks, North Dakota, recently, I met two of the Base Historians at SAC there and they got me the inside skinny on finding all of Bootsy's military records. So now I will proceed to Montgomery, Alabama, and find the best cleanest facts of his military life that I can find.

We always thought he'd come back, with mud from the Amazon on his boots, and bust up school. This hero, this saint, who for me enjoyed the grand theater of never *being* there. I got my idea of the way it was to be a true man, a hero. Be glorious, but don't *be* there. Like all the great dead. They don't have to be there, you really don't want them there. You just hear of them, see an old photo. Cogitate. It is not for nothing what opera the past takes on, because it's not there. He is not there. She is not there. Not only does absence make the heart grow fonder, it makes history your own beautiful lie.

Another photograph I see is of me, myself, just a smiling tiny spoiled brat in baby shoes with my hair parted on the left. Photographs of myself never meant much to me. I'm so vain, for one thing, that no picture ever got it good enough, and on rough days or while I'm working, I don't like anybody with a flashbulb around me. The only camera I own is a twenty-five-dollar Polaroid I bought at a grocery store in Missoula, Montana. I once saw a man set up for a picture of Lake Jenny under the Tetons before he'd even *looked* at the vista. Now that I'm older I like to see some candid shots from the past, but I never needed photographs to remind me of what a good time I had or was, and I'm amazed by people who do. When the shot of me was taken, we were living in Pascagoula, or maybe Long Beach, towns on the Gulf of Mexico. My father and mother—I was a late and surprising birth to my mother, thirty-six, and my father, thirty-eight—were working in the shipyards. The War was on and the battleships and destroyers were underway. Any day, the Japs could hit the beach, my brother Bobby remembers, and all the guys had their air rifles ready.

My mother was furnished rootbeer at the plant where she worked briefly, and can still not bear the taste of the stuff. My dad has the memory of a delicate scholar, and a careful mastery of English that he might have learned early or later, as necessity required in the insurance field, where communication to good and bad old boys trying to read contracts was more important by the voice in simple, plain statement than by small single-spaced print on the page. My father, Bill, went up to Ole Miss to be a lawyer, and roomed with Senator Eastland (a horrible grunting reactionary to me, but to my father just an old pal from the twenties), but Dad had to drop out to support his family back in Homewood. He recalls I could shout out my address, "Seven Leven Resca de la Palma!" at a precocious age, in case I was lost, I guess.

One thing that bored the hell out of me with the late fine writer Truman Capote was that he was always making it perfectly clear what an early genius he was. I saw Truman do this thrice in person, making the same speech for enormous fees at little schools in the South, sucking in the trembling little crowds around where he grew up. Very well, but when I heard it the third time, I got up and left the auditorium at the University of Alabama, having a new definition for jerk. This is rambling just a bit to say that I can't remember doing things except when I was doing them already. I learned to swim by jumping off the pier into deep water, knowing my father was going to save me if I got in trouble. He was out there in the water. Maybe I don't fear much because my father was always out there, in the water, in the brown sea water near Pascagoula. I don't recall ever being unable to swim. I don't recall ever not loving the oceans and the lakes and their mysteries.

Next photograph you see is of my mother and father, and me in the middle with my toy gun. The car behind us, I believe, is a good one, a Mercury, I think. Dad in his pinstripe, Mother lovely in the fashion of the year. The year was 1948, and the picture is significant because we took a lot of trips in good cars. My father came up to Clinton because of my mother's asthmatic condition. The coastal air was ruining her, a doctor said, and she weighed ninety pounds. My dad came to Clinton with $1200 and a penchant for salesmanship. He had sworn never to be poor again. In this old photo it's good to see my mother healthy, too. Clinton was a village of maybe a thousand souls, counting dogs, while I was growing up. Even so, a car hit me on the way to first grade; then the man backed up and ran over me again. This is a joke, which you learn to make when nothing else is happening, reader.

The man was horrified, and all I got out of it was a dislocated thumb, and a sense of death, I suppose. Out cold, black, nothing. I woke up howling with Dr. Reynolds twisting my thumb back into place. My father, to the point, always believed in a good car, and he wanted to know the U.S.A. We traveled. Miami, Quebec, Silver Springs, Florida, where, in the photo, you see my mother and me in the back of one of the famed glass-bottomed boats.

Looking down, you could see enormous schools of blue channel catfish, some of them as big as I was. I thought, naturally, of sneaking in after hours when the wardens were off watch, laying a big worm down there, hauling off a carful of those beauties and arriving home the envy of whatever class I was in. I was always in love and I always wanted to show off. Except for music and writing and learning a little Latin eventually, nothing was fun enough to interest me in school. Mrs. Bunyard, Mrs. King, Mrs. Blackwell, and later Dick Prenshaw, who taught me music fine, straight and pure (I played trumpet) kept me alive. I've never been a thief, but I had an early sense from the Baptist church and the thundering despots associated with the Baptist college in town that whatever pleasure you ever got was stolen.

I keep a deep holy sense of the illicit which I suppose I will ever have. Thanks, Clinton.

Nothing is really that bad when you look back from my distance, and in fact most of it was good. Next photo you see my friends. Rod Flagler, the hip visitor from Culver City, California, is the taller one holding the gun to my side for a gag. The others pictured are Edward Ratliff and Betsy Bell, my playmates, along with John and Billy Quisenberry, unpictured. The picture was taken in Mrs. Caskey's yard. Mrs. Caskey was Rod's grandmother and he was in town for long visits during the summers. It's really hot in deep

Mississippi in the summers, and this was the standard wear for three or four months, in those years of the early fifties when air-conditioners were rare (and television sets were even rarer). We ran around near naked and barefoot, and we could run just about anywhere in town.

There was no crime to speak of. Nobody thought about creeps taking off children. That was a thing far off and terrible in the newspapers, involving the rich or famous, such as the Lindbergh case. We had free roam of, let's say, two square miles, but I recently looked around the town and noticed how tiny the radius was in our neighborhood with its brick streets—"Old Clinton," as they call it now. We played in each other's backyards, and for more adventures we walked up to the college football field and down to the Quisenberry's pecan grove, then sometimes across the tracks to a small forest of pines and oaks, where there was a pipe on a steel cable. You took hold from your perch about twenty feet up, held on to the pipe dearly and slid down stomach-dropping fast until the ride leveled out and you dropped off running. You had to time it right, and let go of the pipe at the exact second, else you'd smash into the oak trunk at high speed, which only dolts ever did. We had one or two black friends, especially "Bunchie," who could throw a baseball fast, hit, and was a solid buddy. Later, the mother of one of my friends—whose racism was appalling to my folks, who wouldn't let Bunchie eat at the kitchen table with me, but let him eat on the back porch—shrieked enough to have Bunchie eliminated from playing baseball with us white kids. Blacks were yard help, maids and garbagemen, and vegetable vendors. I remember the big Negro voice waking you up as the man called out "Corn!" and "Matos!" from his mule-drawn wagon, steel wheelrims clicking on the bricks.

Blacks lived across the tracks. From my old man's garden you could see the tin roofs.

The best thing about my childhood was that I never worried about anything—nothing. I had my toy gun in my hand, and my dog "Dopey"—a halfbreed Eskimo spitz and collie with brown spots on white shaggy hair who lived to be fifteen—buried by my brother Bobby and me in a cardboard box in the old man's garden (it was the first time I ever saw my brother, who was eleven years older than I, weep). My sister Dot named the dog after one of the dwarfs in *Snow White*. He wasn't dumb, and survived three hits by autos before the senile Dr. Eddleman backed over him and finished him. In a *driveway*. I don't bear any grudges, but for godsake, let's keep these ancient numbed-away old farts off the road. Most of them can walk faster than they drive, anyway. Brings up the fact that Mrs. Eddleman, who taught me in junior high, was talking away—history or something—when one of those wild older guys from the country cut a fart that would be a room-emptier at an entire library. We were in a hot, tiny room right above the cafeteria. The guy's name was Jimmy Hooks, I think, and he brought an unloaded .25 revolver with him to class for Show and Tell. Mrs. Eddleman—a short, stout, gracefully educated lady—lifted her breast watch on its chain, looked at the class and sniffed. The monster was hanging about, vile. It wasn't going anywhere for a while. Children were feigning death by gas attack. "Class, now. I believe we should know how to behave when such situations arise," she said.

I should, but I still don't.

I with my toy gun in my hand and my spotter Dopey, we roamed the land and ruled it. I finally set up a Kool-Aid stand and made enough to buy a real Daisy air rifle, with which I shot at sparrows and bluejays and made impossible long shots at crows and buzzards. Thing about a buzzard hovering was to shoot so fast, cocking, recocking, firing around him, that a beebee might with some luck pierce his throat. I doubt anybody on the face of the earth has brought a buzzard down with a Daisy like this, but ammo cost nothing, and when four of us were together, Ratliff with the Daisy pump, which shot like a .22 if you pumped it enough, we thought we'd at least wing one of the great hideous birds, maybe pen it up, and take it to Show and Tell in the fifth grade. Edward Ratliff had more experience with firearms and chemistry than the rest of us. When he was eight he threw a whole pack of .22 shells on the sidewalk until one of them went off and put fragments in his legs. The Ratliffs owned the Chevrolet agency in town, were rather well off, took me on trips to Florida with them. Mr. Ratliff taught me how to cast for bass. He caught big ones, seven and eight pounds. The favorite lure then was the Bayou Boogie. His advice was "Son, just keep throwing and throwing." He bought for his son, Edward the Third, an entire sporting goods store, and there was a nice painted electrified little house behind their big one, where the goods were kept. The Ratliffs had a television earlier than anybody else in Clinton. My mother was a big one for never *imposing* on people. So I sat in a lawnchair and watched Hopalong Cassidy ride on his white horse in his black outfit fringed in white from the vantage of forty yards, with all the power turned up on my binoculars. Clandestinely. If Mother had found out about it, she'd have thought I owed them something. Also it smacked of being a Peeping Tom, which is deplorable. Maybe a certain kind of woman with a Baptist frame of mind is what we can use to survive sometimes. My mother is sweet and kind, and has a heart full of the real Jesus. She cares deeply about beauty. She was a high school teacher when my dad met her. She was a beauty. He had his Buick convertible.

Now my dear mother is seventy-seven, stricken by rheumatoid arthritis. My hair's getting grayer. I pray for her, but I have never heard God speak back. At about fifteen I was driven from the Baptist church by an evangelist who said that he had talked with God last night. You lying fraud, I thought. I had felt holy, I had rededicated my life to Christ three times, but God did not talk to me. I'd never heard a mere phrase from the pulpit, so much that I quit the church.

I played golf as a youngster with a certain minister of the local church who chattered and advised me so much while I was trying to hit the ball that he made me quit the game. The same minister came into our house, saw some of the cut-out pages from *Esquire* magazine, saw them stapled on the wall, none of them even near sexual, and, after eating at my house and receiving the support of my parents, scolded me, almost pointing his finger, telling me to rip my foul pictures off the wall. The same minister counseled brides-to-be about sex so much that it scared them. In fact he was just a greased awful mess. Old times now forgotten, look away, look away, look away, Dixieland. Thing is, I haven't forgot. What I missed from the pulpit was the courage of truth, with no roses and no grease.

Directly across the street from us in the fifties was Mr. Farrell, sitting on his porch. He was a painter by trade and a great adorer of me. He made me a guitar out of a cigar box and rubber bands. He had lost his son in a plane crash near town, right on the college campus, I think, and he and his wife made much of me, in their house and under the spreading arms of live oaks, big gnarled oaks.

I trailed through the woods and the fields, under the pine trees, singing with wind and almost scary, the high witch moan they made. Then my dog and I went across the burned-up cornfields. They had big thick weeds with hard boles at the top. I don't know the botanical name, but these sticks made perfect spears. They were balanced perfectly and they sailed way high even from my small arm. They'd come down and stick in the ground. Dopey and I covered the turf, the whole environs. Then we played with Rod, Betsy, Edward, and the Quisenberry brothers. Sometimes there was a bigger guy, Tommy Poates, a little more violent at touch football than most of us thought the rules called for. Tommy's a pal of mine, maybe a Bird Colonel in the Air Force now, or something. You get over old injuries, grow up, and are glad the guy is on *our* side. John Quisenberry is a lawyer in Los Angeles now, and a Commander in the Naval Reserve, having been a pilot and hero in Vietnam. I have written of him, have borrowed from his experience like mad, and in horribly drunken moments (long forgotten, I hope) I have told others I *was* him. It was the Bootsy and the booze in me.

Rod Flagler, precocious and tall and blond, aided by his odd accent, which is whatever Californian is, brought plastic models—just the castaway hulls, really—of battleships and destroyers with him. His father worked for Revell Plastics in Culver City. We used them to set up surrealistic towns made from shoeboxes, with the boats right in the main street. We had plastic soldiers and cowboys, Indians. At that time there were no models of black fighting Marines, but we'd have loved to put them in there too. All the citizens—I mean really the soldiers, since plastic models of decent citizens standing about came late and bored me when they came—milled about in attitudes of readiness. For two days we would construct the cardboard town, painting windows on, cutting out doors, folding shirt cardboards for the roofs. Then we would hang back and observe the town, this fascinating little place on the bare ground in the cool shade of Mrs. Caskey's backyard.

Then on the next day, it was time and we would bring out a box of the old Diamondhead matches. We didn't want to do anything as simple and child-ish as set fire to the place. The town was too pretty for that. It was Flagler who introduced the matchshooter to us. You make them out of old-fashioned wooden clothespins with the spring on them. When this spring is taken off and reversed, you deepen the notch so that when you snap it, the head of the match, inserted between the heads of the pin, is ignited and thrown out in a considerable arc. It's a smoking rocket that flares about the time it reaches the little town, explodes and flames. So you wanted to eventually burn the town, but what you wanted most was the art of the destruction. Otherwise, you could moisten the end of the match, strike it, and sail it, so that it would leave a smoking trail as stirring as in the lines of the National Anthem. The town and boats and citizens would be set on fire, certainly, but it might take all afternoon if you stood off ten feet and did it the sporting way.

Literary influences are generally tedious to me, especially as revealed by writers drooling about their precious boy- and girlhoods. Yes, we were once little, and now we are big. Certain things happened when we were very little or medium little. Very well. As a bias, I am more interested in what hap-pened to you yesterday, strictly yesterday. Still, only a jerk lies about what he really is, and my fascination with the military, the artfully destructive, began early. We kids in the rural village of Clinton invented our own movies. Otherwise, there was only the radio and the Hilltop Theater—twenty-five cents for two movies, popcorn, and a drink, on Saturday afternoons. I got a quarter for mowing our lawn (pushmower), and struck out for bliss in moving pictures. On the radio were "Straight Arrow," "The Green Hornet," and "The Shadow."

We searched out Reds and Nazis, who were lurking like mad behind thick bushes and in some people's basements. We had rubber guns, we made a cannon out of a pipe that shot flashlight batteries, using an M-80 firecracker as the charge. We made a catapult that threw a tin can off a bent-down chinaberry trunk. Thing would travel over with a lit cherry bomb in it and you had a hell of a grenade launcher. When we were older we got into beebee gun fights. It's a miracle nobody lost an eye, as my friend the poet Jim Seay did, over at Batesville—shot by a young air-riflist.

But Bootsy was always there. My uncle was always there, present because he was so gone. I expected to see his plane come in over the cedars, the pines, the oaks, the magnolias, his plane permanently on fire but surviving. And he would, with his laugh, smoke coming off his jacket, be Captain America, my unc. He was with me and us as we ran barefoot through mud, stubble, stickers, past the cane growing tall and green, and we climbed into the tree house in Mrs. Harrison's yard. The tree house was stocked with comic books, our first library. Mrs. Harrison was doing her vain best to teach me piano.

The last photograph I bring attention to is that of my great-grandfather Chatham, at a reunion for Confederate veterans in Biloxi. He's standing near the palmettos of Beauvoir, homesite of Jefferson Davis. I love the cane, the coat, the mustache, the style. I never saw or knew the man. He was a Captain of infantry in the C.S.A. I adore the fine look of the old fellow. He fought the good fight against what they thought was strictly a blasphemous invasion from the North.

Clinton was only thirty miles east of Vicksburg, the town Grant conquered, to break the back of the Confederate Army in the West. Whenever there was a trip to take, a "field trip," our class went over to Vicksburg to view the grand, rolling, deep green battlefields. And it is a holy, haunted place, haunted by the soldiers buried and the bronze busts of the generals in coves of gloom around twilight. *Spooky* is the quality I recall. I wouldn't want to be there come dark, unless with a pack of kids.

So I had the Civil War in my blood and read the books about it—Catton's, Foote's, Watkins' "Co. Aytch"—but the old hideous conflict was in me long before I got to the libraries.

I was talking with my father, who's eighty-two now, and he was remarking what a horrible thing it was, how could it have happened? That anyone could get Americans to line up against, charge, and shoot each other? "It was leadership we needed, son. Leadership, men who could stop this terrible thing happening, our boys killing each other." My old man is a great reader and spends his winters—afflicted with painful arthritic feet and near stone deafness—reading books and books. The old man always wanted to *know*, to know things true, solid, the inside skinny.

Barry Hannah

Well despite the small civil wars that occurred between Father and Mother and Son, until I was, say, thirty-nine, and we all just called them off, I'm glad the war's been won for peace of mind for all of us, and great God, I want to thank the Old Goat right now for giving me the need to know things—things true, solid, the inside skinny.

Then I can start lying again and make a living.

I GOT
A HORN,
YOU GOT
A HORN

ELLEASE SOUTHERLAND

Although I was born in the North, in a small hospital near Sheepshead Bay, Brooklyn, New York, the South was more than an equal presence in my girlhood years. My two older brothers had been born in Florida, our father's birthplace. The South as a state of mind, the black South with its sometimes latent but unmistakable ties to Africa, would shape our lives. Papa was Papa, not the more citified daddy. And I, as first sister, was called Sister, the same as my Georgia-born cousin Thomasina and my Grand-aunt Marie. We said yes sir, when answering our father, and yes ma'am, when answering our mother. Never mind all those around us answering a simple yes or no; we were in this world, but not of this world. In my upbringing, respect for older adults bordered on reverence. Respect for authority recalled the moments when my father stepped down from a Southern sidewalk to let whites pass. There was no "back talk" in our house and back talk had a definition broad enough to include insolent looks and simple questioning; this repression another reflection of Southern racialism; a repression I would find recorded in the slave narrative by Frederick Douglass and in William Wells Brown's *Clotel*.

Most of my Northern neighbors were Southern-born. The Davises next door raised chickens. From our kitchen window I watched their drunken father run down a hen who had just laid an egg and, in panic, the flustered hen circled back to stomp the egg before running off again. A dead chicken hanging from the shower in their bathroom would become an image in my first novel. With the exception of that image and the stomped egg, the neighbors' chickens didn't bother us; we rose with the sun and retired close to sunset. It was barely dusk when we lay in bed on summer evenings, listening to other children still rambling up and down the metal-plated steps. We drifted to sleep while they were still outside at play.

Perhaps even the size of the family was Southern-influenced; we were farm-size, eventually a family of fifteen. My father spoke often of the five brothers and father working the turpentine woods of Florida, lugging buckets of gum so heavy he felt it stunted his growth; all that to earn a combined salary so meager that it barely kept food on the table. Just in his early teens, my father, an outstanding math student, had been pulled from school to suffer an entire year of hard labor.

I would not set foot in the South until age twenty-three. As I stood on Miami Beach, I looked past the palm trees, the sand and the water, and into earlier years when my father could not stand there; he wore an identification card with a photograph sharp enough to show every blemish on his skin. Then the only blacks allowed on certain beaches were blacks who were employed. But long before my visit, my father's sermons gave Florida a presence in my life, recalling boyhood years on the docks heading shrimp with both hands, an eight-year-old so skillful and quick that a Portuguese sailor would take him out on a boat where my father would head shrimp before they reached the docks. The boat ran into an eight-day storm that would become a recurring metaphor in my father's sermons. The wooden floors he scrubbed to surprise his mother also appeared in sermons so frequently that I felt the rough clean surface. My father's parents, especially Grandmamma, would visit many times, traveling more than a thousand miles, bringing the sun with her, bringing euphoria to the cold-water flat rented for thirteen dollars a month and later to the steam-heated house in Queens. She showed me how to make biscuits, how to test the rising power of baking powder. She showed me how to cut a butterfly sleeve and examined my sewing. My mother confided in me years later that her mother-in-law was in many ways nicer to her than her own mother. Grandmother told me story after story, beginning with "back in my home town." I would need her narrative voice to open my novel.

I Got a Horn, You Got a Horn

My father, Monroe Penrose, first right, with three of his brothers. From left, LausDeo, Isaiah, Jimmy (a friend), and Brother Mac.

Ellease Southerland

A small toy frying pan hanging from a nail on the kitchen wall formed another Southern connection. Although I was usually careful with things, I could not convince my mother to let me touch it, not once. It was the toy she played with in North Carolina. In this family where almost nothing she had was exclusively hers, the frying pan was all hers. That pan recalled the open field, the moment a cow walked toward the five-year-old who would become my mother, and the sight of the large brown eyes looking directly into her eyes sent her running, running to the arms of an old woman who was gentle and sensitive, a woman she called Mamma Habersham. She would give my mother water from the bell of a cow to cure her stuttering. She was the protective spirit during my mother's formative years, in the years when five cents could buy a bucket of milk. Many days I glanced at the toy pan, anxious to hold it, just once. But I was soon to have something special, all my own.

On a mid-morning in June 1948, I awoke to a world filled with bright sun. It was a vanilla morning rich with bakery smells floating back to the room where I lifted my head, awed that the eighteenth had finally come: it

Paternal grandmother, Valerie C. Southerland, on one of many visits.

was my birthday and I was five years old. My brother Lorenzo, a noisy three-year-old, shared the large crib. And every evening when the family gathered to sing, we shared the same voice, tenor. Monroe, whom we called Brother, sang soprano, and LausDeo, the oldest, sang alto. We harmonized in the cluttered kitchen standing near the blackboard. After a series of exercises to strengthen our lungs and diaphragms, after facing walls and doors, pushing against the immovable surfaces to develop the lungs, then reversing and pushing again, and then blowing a piece of paper dangling from a string, blowing with a hard steady stream of breath, we finally stood together, hands cupped to sing "O Mary Don't You Weep," "I Heard the Preaching of the Elders," we sang "O Where You Running Sinner," we sang the *solfeggio* for "Onward Christian Soldiers," and we sang "I Got a Robe, You Got a Robe," and Grandpapa, visiting from Florida, put on his imaginary robe and began to prance about the kitchen. Brother sang of the crown, and Grandpapa put on the crown. We watched fascinated. We had never seen our father act so playful, especially with a church song. "I got shoes, you got shoes," Lorenzo and I sang out, and watched him bend to put on imaginary shoes, he winked at us and then walked "all over God's heaven." "I got a horn, you got a horn," LausDeo's alto called. "All God's children got a horn!"

In the world outside, they were singing "Old Man River" and "Irene, Good Night." Just humming a few notes of these songs could get you a heavy warning, a sudden slap, or a full-fledged whipping which was routine in our house, leaving me too many nights with painful lumps in my throat as I cried internally, because my father's heavy voice blasted my nervous system. Or because he beat my bigger brothers. For what? For not singing loud enough. For letting their minds wander. For lollygagging. For some imagined mischief. For being boys. To break their male spirits in a world that could lynch them for being black and magnificent and male. He pulled them by the head, and before all of us, bent them between his knees, buttocks exposed and whipped them with a leather strap.

No wonder I had threatening dreams many nights. In the dark, long after the clock stopped ticking, a shadowy form approached the crib. It stood still a moment, then leaned its face close to mine. My parents asleep in the same room, on the other side of the curtain, seemed too distant to save me. Only Lorenzo knew the long moments when a threatening form approached the crib, stood perfectly still, leaned its face close to ours, then turned and went away.

In the morning, we told the big brothers; we had seen the boogeyman.

"What?" Brother's eyes brimmed with amusement.

"We did."

"There's no such thing."

"Didn't we, Lorenzo?"

"Um, yeah!"

The big brothers laughed wantonly, falling over each other.

Grandpapa, Thomas Monroe Southerland, in his carriage. St. Augustine, Florida.

"What did he look like?" LausDeo asked, still smiling. His skin was lighter than mine. But we had the same slanted eyes and full lips.

"He had a light bulb on his back."

They laughed senselessly, tears spilling from their dark eyes. When they controlled themselves long enough to speak, they asked, "What did he do?"

"He looked into our faces," I said.

"Then he went to the bathroom," Lorenzo added.

"That wasn't the boogeyman. That was Papa!" They destroyed themselves. They laughed themselves into pure ruin while I stood thin-legged and serious, puzzled. I wanted to join them, the two brothers born in Florida. When I was just a pile of cells in my mother's womb, they were already a complete fraternity, talking together. Now they went to school, together. They knew how to place calls from the public telephones. They could cross the street.

Monroe and LausDeo, my older brothers, Florida-born. Background, kitchen blackboard.

And they could tell time. Neither of them ever hit me and Deo didn't really tease me. But Brother! He once said that I would eventually resemble a certain wrinkled old woman whose hanging clothes had an odor of snuff and my grief was complete. Yet I treasured him more than anyone. He boxed the neighborhood bullies who bothered me. And of course I would marry him since he was named after my father and I named after my mother; Monroe marries Ellease. It was just a fact which I did not discuss, not even with him. Years later he would patiently teach me algebra, spending more than an hour every day that summer, out in the yard, under the grape arbor. At thirteen, I would get a 99 as a final grade, because of him. But when I was five, he came home from school gripping his hand with blood oozing from a rip. He had torn his hand on barbed wire.

"Why did you climb the fence?" Mamma asked him.

Peroxide foamed in the jagged cut.

"I wanted to pick some flowers for you."

He had to have stitches, but he didn't cry. Perhaps it was because he never cried that my father beat him harder and longer trying to make him cry. The tears would come in his adult years. Why are there so many beatings in this story? a creative writing professor would ask years later. His question was rhetorical, but in a quiet moment, I would have to answer. I would recall the day an elementary school teacher said your brothers are too quiet. You talk enough, Ellease, but your brothers are too quiet.

But in June 1948 I had a day of absolute joy. Mamma gave me my first pocketbook, a white plastic shoulder bag with a zipper. Inside was a handkerchief and two pennies. And shortly after the big brothers went off to school, and while Papa was in the bakery decorating a cake for me, Mamma, Lorenzo and I went outside where the narrow street of tenements became beautiful, showered in sun. Something down the street caught my eye, but I was aware of my mother's soft hand shading the viewer of the camera; I heard the shutter's soft click.

Less than three months later, after the summer had come and gone and the brothers were off to school again, and I stood at the closed door long after their footsteps disappeared into the autumn hours, Mamma cleared a place at the kitchen table and called me. She handed me a brand-new notebook and a long yellow, well-sharpened pencil. I could hardly breathe. She pressed the book open, and printed the alphabet across the top of the page. Her stomach rested against me as she watched my hand. It was just what I needed. How did she know? First the pocketbook, now a notebook! The days shortened. Before winter, I was spelling everything in sight. And there was so much in sight. Cardboard boxes with clothes stacked against a kitchen wall, the boxes which Grandmother (maternal) cited when calling the apartment a dilapidated dump and a pig pen. I read those boxes, c-o-f-f-e-e, being my favorite, with its double *f* and double *e*. I read the boxes on the table.

"Whose that?" I asked about the man on the oatmeal box.

"A Quaker."

"Quaker?"

"Yes. Quakers helped slaves escape on the underground railroad." I envisioned the subway as Mamma spoke of children my age and Lorenzo's, who could be caught and sold into slavery. Our father's oldest aunts were slaves. His mother, my grandmother, had just escaped slavery. The round-faced Quakers had white beards and dark hats; they had secrets of slavery. The

Ellease at five, with white shoulder bag, and brother Lorenzo. Background, bakery window.

baby Tommie, seated in his highchair, quietly sucked his thumb, his thick long braids brushed his shoulders while I absorbed this history. It was dangerous to be white, I reasoned, because too many white people would go to hell because of this slavery wickedness.

I had heard the scriptures, read every morning, six mornings a week in prayer meeting. I heard sermons preached twice on Sundays. We dressed and went from 26 Thatford Avenue to "the church" at 28 Thatford Avenue. There Papa described the ancient lepers and the modern sexually promiscuous, the beauty of old temples, the madness of ancient kings and the bloody battles. His orderly sense of composition was shaped by thirteen years in school, including a year of college. But his sermons also rang in a Southern sing-song voice, closer to song than to speech. His own secrets hidden in Bible stories of stonings and sex, his eyes pressed shut, his voice rasping in his throat, pressure changed his face, distress slit his eyes. And I eventually believed him when he said it's hard to be a Christian. At first it didn't seem hard at all, unless you counted the wooden folding chairs that numbed my hips, or the long wait before we could go and eat the macaroni and cheese with cubes of seasoned ham tucked into the melted cheese. Or drink cocoa. Or have rice and gravy so delicious that you didn't really need the chicken. That part was hard, but not so hard as being thrown to the lions—a man, his wife and all their children, thrown to the lions! All right. If it was that hard to be a Christian, then I wouldn't try to be a Christian. And I wouldn't be a sinner. I would be in between. After I made that decision, the very next Sunday, Papa preached a sermon entitled "The Plight of the Neutral Christian." He read his text. Something about God would take you if you were hot or if you were cold, but if you were lukewarm he would spew you out. Papa gave the etymologies of the words in his text. He gave his illustration of *neutral*, like clear nail polish, the polish my mother put on her stockings to stop a run. I wished I could put some on my nails. Then he gave the final truth: the neutral Christian, he said, goes straight to hell. I was outdone.

Christmas of that same year, I wrote my own letter to Santa Claus. I asked for rice. That was an easy word to spell. And for a doll. But when it came to carriage, I had to humbly ask the help of my oldest brother. But Santa Claus didn't bring the carriage and I could not be consoled. A note on the kitchen blackboard read: sorry kids, santa can't read so good. The Christmas dinner, the candy, spinning tops, doll and other small toys could not take the disappointment from my eyes. Only an explanation could have done the trick. It would be two years later when Grandmamma (maternal) would buy two carriages, one for Ruthie, and one for me.

The huge school building rescued me from the shabby apartment. Public School 84, with its tall brick walls and many classrooms, became a sanctuary. But school was more than books.

The school yard rang with verbal abuse.

"Your mother wears combat boots."

"You ain't got none."

"Basket!"

"Oooow!" the school children called.

A basket? What's wrong with a basket, I wondered.

"Your father drinks sneaky pete."

"You ain't got none."

"What are you doing at that door?" a teacher asked a boy.

"I'm a guard," he said.

A god! I repeated to myself and wondered at his wickedness. His blasphemy.

Summer seemed to interrupt school fun. Summer seemed too long except for the days when we went to the park or to the beach. If Uncle Ike, my father's brother, didn't drive us, we took the bus and train. We liked getting caught in sudden showers, or being pressed in subway crowds, cautioned to hold on to the pole. Leaving the house, however, was a risky, exciting business. Papa tore open two long loaves of bread.

"Slap that mayonnaise on one side, son," he told Deo. Then he put another slice on top and impressed us; both sides had mayonnaise. The vinegar smells stinging our noses, our mouths watered as the dozens of baloney and liverwurst sandwiches piled up. Brother wrapped them in wax paper and they were stored in canvas shopping bags. Papa put a big hunk of ice in a tin can, added sugar and checked to be sure he had several packets of Kool-Aid.

"Hurry up, Honey," he always said rather impatiently.

"I'm coming dear," Mamma said. But she took more time.

"Either we get going, or we call the whole thing off."

We got uneasy.

But finally the doors were locked and we were on our way to the Rockaway Avenue bus stop.

As expected, the bus driver counted as we climbed aboard, one . . . two . . . three . . . My parents didn't have to pay for me, not even when I was six;

I was no bigger than a four-year-old. But even then, we were humiliated by the many passengers who counted us and who in their careful counting discounted us.

"All those yours?" a spontaneous spokesperson always asked.

A smile and almost imperceptible nod from our parents confirmed suspicions.

"God bless you."

"Thank you."

They ought to stop, Grandmother always said. You need to put a lock on it, she said. I wondered about such a lock.

Picnic at Prospect Park.

Even after we were cautiously seated at the back of the bus, some turned to further examine us. We were at their mercy until the day we caught a man recounting, using his finger to help him, one . . . two . . . three . . . We joined him in low intent voices, four . . . five, six. He looked into our eyes. He looked away. And we were free to think about the long stretches of grass at Prospect Park, the long picnic table where Papa would spread the cloth. He would stand, magnificent in the shade, wearing a broad-brimmed hat and cotton shirt, our father who had studied Latin and French. He was the ice-cream maker. Each morning he lifted a heavy rock, his arm muscles bulged jagged as the rock. He hauled the two-gallon can with sugar and ice. He added park water to make sweet cherry drinks which reminded us of sermons that dreamed of joy and feasting. We were his children. He wouldn't take a million dollars for any of us, he'd said. He served us paper cups filled with cherry drink. We chewed the delicious baloney sandwiches. We gulped our icy cold drinks, close to miserable with happiness.

Then late one July afternoon, it seemed that we might never picnic again. We all ate silently at the rough wooden table in the kitchen. Afternoon light fell gently across our moist faces as we ate from bent pie tins a hot meal of

Another summer picnic.

home baked beans seasoned with brown sugar, tomatoes and onions. We had thick hominy grits that hit the plate with a solid, threatening thump that said eat all that stuff. Papa served, and we had better eat it all too, because he was in no mood for foolishness. Half the people in the world were starving. We had frankfurters sliced the long way and turned face down to make it look like whole frankfurters. We secretly promised ourselves that when we grew up we would have whole frankfurters. In the meantime we ate the half. Our father solemnly chewed and swallowed. Our mother suckled the seventh baby, William Ira. Then seemingly without warning, LausDeo's head snapped back on his neck. His mouth fell open, he appeared to grin and wallop! Papa dealt him a sobering slap. "Quit fooling around at the table, son."

But Mamma jumped to her feet, handing the baby to me, putting her breast back into her blouse. She called Brother. "Telephone the hospital." Brother shook a nickel from the royal blue glass pig and hurried to the candy store. We soon heard footsteps. Police. Ambulance. Neighbors crowded the hall and kitchen.

"Your brother is never going to walk again," a neighbor told me. "He has polio."

See? See what happens when there are too many people in one family? You wear old-fashioned clothes, knickerbockers and short rubber boots that snap on the side. You should wear tall boots that zip, or get your feet wet, or stay home. They examined our humble home, the clutter of the darkened bedrooms. Eventually they left. And in the following days I wondered who would help Brother to carry the shopping bags when we went on picnics. Who would help hold the children's hands when we boarded the train? The doctors don't know what's wrong, Mamma explained. But before August ended, Deo came home, walking, eating a store-bought ice-cream cone. He wore old fashioned knickers and a plaid short-sleeved shirt. His skin was paler, but he smiled shyly, embarrassed as we kept hugging him and hugging him. He was slightly unsteady, but standing. He would be running and chasing squirrels when summer rolled around again.

They went to the beach without Ruthie and me one weekend in winter; we were at Grandmother's house. She had taken Mamma and Papa to court, but I knew nothing about that then. She had described us eating from pie tins. We used proper plates on Sundays only. When I was six, I just knew that Friday was my lucky day, because my grandmother came every Friday and kept me and Ruthie for the weekend. In her spacious seven-room apartment

I Got a Horn, You Got a Horn

My sister Ruth Eleanor with our parents at Prospect Park.

Another summer, another picnic.

LausDeo in knickers on a school visit to La Guardia Airport.

on the corner of Throop and Putnam, we had scrambled eggs and real butter for breakfast. We had milk from the container. We heard the radio sing "pack up your troubles in your old kit bag and smile," and we took warm baths every night. If only Grandmother didn't give us a fingerful of thick camphorated oil to swallow on winter nights. If only she didn't talk about Mamma so much, it would have been perfect.

But she kept on talking. I said if my daughter has one more baby I'm going to leave town. I told her one baby is enough baby. I told her two would do. I told her three is enough for me I told her four and no more. She's so stubborn.

"Look at the sweaters she put on this child," she said one Friday evening. "One sweater, Lord have mercy." She removed the sweater from Ruthie's up-

The brothers at Coney Island in winter.

stretched arms. "Two sweaters, Lord have mercy . . . three sweaters, Lord have mercy. Four!" There were five sweaters finally resting on the pile and Grandmother asked for another round of mercy.

"She wants to be sure they're warm," Mrs. Miller, the elderly listener, said.

I stood by, silent. I knew the pain in my mother's eyes when she heard her mother's loud voice broadcasting on the front steps. Some foolish neighbors laughed. They had four, five or as many children, but they laughed.

One other event sobered me those otherwise perfect weekends: those Saturdays at noon, when the siren sounded and reminded me of the chain around my neck, my name and address stamped in metal, a metal which would not burn, or be dissolved in blood. The brooding sound rang over my world as an ocean grieving over drowned bodies from Africa. My mother had described Germany's ovens, the gas chambers where millions were put to death. I would not have believed the brutality of slavery, I would not have believed the brutality of Germany, if my mother had not told me.

But Grandmother's house was a security against those pains. The back rooms were rented and Ruthie and I were not to go back there and bother the Bradshaws; yet they often called us and gave us presents. Grandpapa slept in a small room, a large foyer between the living room and the dining room. He had glass-doored bookcases and boxes of photographic equipment. I didn't know he was my mother's second stepfather. He was simply Grandpapa, a fair-skinned man with gray hair and a matching bushy mustache. He said I had such nice straight legs. That I had a bushy head of hair, which he rumpled so playfully. And he gave me a handful of chocolate-covered peanuts. It didn't seem unusual to me that Grandmamma and Grandpapa slept in separate beds. Ruthie and I slept with her on a pull-out couch in the living room.

Grandmother bought us new coats, new shoes and new dresses, new straw hats for Easter. Every Sunday morning, we went with her to AME Zion Church, where thousands filled the downstairs pews and we sat in the balcony, across from the Gospel Choir where Grandmother sang. For many years, she had sung on radio. Thousands knew her voice. Thousands awoke early on Sunday mornings to hear Madame Dozier sing, accompanied by her daughter Ellease, playing the piano in an unheated studio where the icy piano keys numbed her fingers. In the big church, now, the maroon rug softened my footsteps. The dark wooden walls, stained glass and cushioned pews, the gleaming pipes of the great organ took the agony out of church. Here four choirs sang: the Youth in white, the Intermediates in wine, the Anthem in green and the Gospel Choir in black. There were forty-four voices in that choir, voices of gray-haired people who scrubbed and ironed all week, who stood as doormen, or worked as janitors and cooks, the people who left the South to make a livelihood in the North, these people sang together. After the other three choirs had sung, the Gospel Choir was the last to rise, to inspire their pastor, Reverend Carrington. Professor Bridges at the organ signaled them and they rose as a single body, the sound of their rising was memorable. They held their sheet music, their tired backs now straight. And when they sang, "Now let us sing till the power of the Lord comes down," the power came down. Grandmother pushed her rugged rhythmic contralto forcing the sopranos into full strength, making the tenors go full stretch as they stayed with her. The bass worked, those old seasoned men turned those deep corners until Brother Emmanuel downstairs, his wavy hair brushed close to his head, hollered, "Help your self, just help your self."

During the prayer that followed, Grandmother quietly took Ruthie, two years old, in her arms; she unzipped her pocketbook, took out a banana,

Maternal grandmother, Ruth Evangeline Dozier Sisco, Madame Dozier to those who heard her Sunday morning broadcasts.

peeled it and broke off portions which she fed Ruthie. I watched this scene with one eye closed. I was too big to eat in church. Years later, back in our father's storefront in Jamaica, Queens, I would open my eyes again to catch Ruthie rapidly chewing hot buttered cornbread during the prayer. She took the food from her pocketbook. And smiling to myself I thought "who steals *her* purse, steals trash."

When Grandmother returned us home on Sunday nights there was usually some tension, some reminder that she had asked a judge for custody on weekends and that custody was granted until the family moved to larger living quarters. One Sunday when Papa ordered everyone to bed, Ruthie wouldn't leave Grandmother's arms, so she undressed her.

"Say your prayers," Papa ordered.

I fell to my knees trembling and hurried through the Lord's Prayer. When I got up, Ruthie was still in Grandmother's arms. Papa yanked her away from Grandmother, threw her to the floor and lashing her with the leather strap ordered, "Say, Our Father."

Crying, Ruthie repeated.

"Who art in heaven." He lashed her back again.

She repeated. She was two years old.

"Hallowed be thy name." He lashed her again.

The words were barely repeated before he yanked her from the floor, carrying her by one arm and tossed her into the crib.

"You beat that baby just because she loves me," Grandmother said.

"Mommie, please leave," Mamma said.

And Grandmother gathered her things and left.

Less than a year later, we did move, eight children and two parents.

The day we moved, Lorenzo and I abused the humble apartment. We stomped the floor. We threw torn newspapers to the floor and spit on it. Our mother said don't do that. She swept the kitchen and left the house clean. She left me with an image that would last an eternity.

Our house on Union Hall Street in Jamaica, Queens, had steam heat and a modern bathroom. The backyard, all ours, had honeysuckles and grapevines. Ruthie and I had our own bedroom. We no longer saw Grandmother. Often when Ruthie prayed, the earlier memory sprang to life, until listening carefully one night, I heard her say:

> And forgive us our debts
> As we forgive our dentist . . .

I Got a Horn, You Got a Horn

In addition to four bedrooms, the new house had porch windows which the family artists filled with posters: Let not your heart be troubled, ye believe in God, believe also in me. . . . Lay up your treasures in heaven where neither moth nor rust doth corrupt nor thieves break through and steal. The printed verses attracted the Jehovah's Witnesses. They came and argued with my father for hours. Dr. Nightingale said the posters ruined the neighborhood, as though that pronouncement would influence my father to remove them.

I was nine years old, living in a nicer neighborhood. I did skip rope on Thatford Avenue, running the block from end to end, finding big billboards advertising beer on every corner. But I was stopped when a small boy from another block, without warning, punched me in the stomach and sent me walking home, doubled over. But in these quieter Jamaica streets, with Joan who lived across the street and Willie Mae and Mattie Bell who lived two houses down, I could jump double dutch for a thousand years and still stay hungry for the crisp rhythm of fast turning ropes. Hopping and turning, breathless with joy. Fancy dancing. Dancing? I was certainly not allowed to dance; John the Baptist lost his head because of dancing. In secret I tried to dance, positive that I would be phenomenal. After all, I had just ridden a

Backyard photograph, Queens.

Before house on Union Hall Street. Background, posters in windows.

bicycle for the first time in my life, discovered that I was perfectly balanced and that I would not fall. But I would be twenty-one before I took my first real dance steps. But before then, some said my size made it easy for me to jump rope. And I was small, small enough to share the toilet seat with Ruthie whenever we had to go to the bathroom at the same time. And we often did, until Papa opened the bathroom door one day and called Mamma to come and see us perched like two birds on the toilet. Mamma closed the door saying, "Mon, please," chiding him for invading our privacy.

At age eleven, all I could do was dream of dancing in a house with no radios, no records, no dancing. The Teenagers would write their own song, "Why Do Fools Fall in Love?" I would be inspired and impressed because they had written the song themselves. But that was outside my world. Inside, my father watched me closely.

"Do you have a slip on under that dress, daughter?"

"Yes sir."

Or, "Daughter, don't let the socket show," he said complaining about the length of my dress, referring to the back of the leg behind the knee.

Late one morning I disappeared briefly to visit my double dutch partner, Joan. When I returned home, my father called.

"Sister?"

"Yes sir!"

He stood in the small corner near the kitchen door, holding a bowl in his arms, mixing something.

"Where were you?"

"Across the street, at Joan's house."

"You didn't tell anybody?"

"No sir. I just went for a few minutes."

His eyes flickered dangerously. "Listen to me carefully," he said. He lifted one hand in a gesture that could end in a slap. "Boys your brother's age," he said, "can get you pregnant and you'll be sticking off!" He rounded an imaginary, enlarged belly. "You'll be with child and nobody, nobody, will want you . . ." His lowered voice became more intense, uncomfortably intimate. "Your aunt was seventeen and never married. She's done rather well, she's got her master's degree, but nobody wants to marry a girl who's been in trouble, do you understand?"

"Yes sir," I said. My scalp was tight. A great heat seemed to burn in my genital tissues. But even in that moment of shocked confusion I disliked his finding the first excuse to gossip about my aunt.

"Don't tell your brothers," he said, before he let me go.

"Yes sir," I said. But I soon whispered to Brother and Deo. To my surprise, they said they had figured that out long ago. I was genuinely amazed at them.

Months later, Mamma mysteriously took me to the bathroom and closed the door. Seated on the side of the tub, she asked, "What is a sign of life?"

"Water?"

"Yes," she said, "but also blood."

"A husband . . . " Mamma continued, searching for a delicate way to describe sexual intercourse, "a husband can hold you naked in his arms."

That sounded rather nice.

My parents said nothing when I gave nature a helping hand; I stuffed my bra with stockings. I did see the look of amusement that passed between them. They also permitted me to straighten my hair. Ten years later, the Black Arts movement would give me back my soft woolen hair. But I was fourteen. Following Brother's footsteps, I too would be Valedictorian of my ninth-grade

Ellease Southerland

Ellease with baby brother Ahomeka.

class. I had already ignored the eighth-grade science teacher, Mr. McCormick, who approached my seat at the beginning of the term and advised, "Don't try to be as good as your brother." Monroe had been his student, consistently earning 98s or 100s. The same teacher did look at me with new respect when I received a 92 on his midterm. The ninth-grade teacher, Mr. Gershoff, would be, in contrast, absolutely supportive and I would earn the science medal that year.

I was fourteen when I got my menses; at fourteen I realized that babies did not exit through the navel, but through the vagina! I was even more amazed at my mother, more appreciative and protective.

I had reached her physical height, 5'2". I put my arms around her the day I found her crying in the vestibule.

"Why don't you leave him?" I asked.

"How can I do that?" she asked.

"You didn't know what he was like when you married him?"

"I knew," she said gently.

Then *I* knew. She married him because she loved him. She knew he was damaged, but she loved him. In many moments we seemed more co-mothers than mother and daughter.

Through the years the family trio had grown. We had become a full chorus and a brass band. The Sunday Papa heard us play religious songs with toy instruments, a Christmas drum, harmonica and xylophone, he said Well! If they can do that with toys, what would they do with the real thing?

Off he went on his bicycle and returned home with a shopping bag full of unpolished, dusty-smelling, dented horns picked up at pawnshops. He emptied the clanking horns onto the living room sofa. A battered French horn, two trombones, three trumpets, cymbals. Drums would follow. Newer horns would follow. Ever since Mamma read to me the newspaper article about Louie Armstrong blowing his trumpet in Africa, I wanted a horn. I had never said anything. It was just something I thought about. At first the valves stuck and the only sound was our frustrated breath. We elaborately wiped our lips and examined the horns as though something sinister held back the sound. We shook the horns as though loosening the sound. Brother (Monroe) made the first peep of a note, then sustained a full-bodied tone. Kiss the horn, he told us, and we were on our way. Neighbors would leave their televisions. Neighbors would sit out on their porches many summer evenings and listen to us rehearse.

I took three children for medical checkups one late spring day. A clinic doctor who did not know the family looked at me suspiciously; at seventeen I appeared to be twelve, maybe thirteen.

"All these are *not* yours," she said.

"No. I'm the oldest sister."

"How many are there?"

"Thirteen."

She shook her head in reproach.

Back home, Mamma cared for her miracle baby, Takwa Fida, the thirteenth. On a Tuesday after school, when I first saw her, her miniature pink hand grabbed the tip of my fingers. The other softer than velvet hand rested

Ellease Southerland

Four on trumpet: Ellease, Naomi, Valerie, James.

Five brothers with horns.

Lorenzo, Thomas, Monroe, Ellease, and Ruth: five of the Brass Chorus,
AME Zion Church, Brooklyn.

on the blanket. I looked at each tiny finger. Her eyes opened momentarily, then closed. There were faint traces of eyebrows to be. Tiny lashes lined her eyes. Her curly blue-black hair was soft as her skin. Even as I restrained the impulse to check her feet for toes, as though responding to my unspoken wish, she poked a perfect foot through the folds of the fluffy blanket. The doctor had first said Mamma had a tumor, then accused her of trying to abort the baby, and eventually discovered that she had a damaged kidney; he recommended removal of both the kidney and the fetus. But working with one kidney, Mamma carried and delivered the baby who would grow up in another bigger house, with a barn, rabbit hutch, garage, four pear trees and an L-shaped grape arbor, all in one hundred square yards, where she would play in two swimming pools, one plastic, bought from the store, the other dug by her father and brothers. The house with its sunporches and larger rooms, the big sprawling yard, was a welcome change. But the religious restrictions never changed.

Sunday afternoons rolled around with claustrophobic regularity. In the

Ellease in big yard at 106th Avenue.

Children's Hour, we sang, played our instruments and reported on our lives in Christ during the past week. We were born wicked and had to keep an eye on ourselves. We had to fast and pray, deny ourselves. It was a religion that seemed to ask us to low-rate ourselves. And William, the seventh, the one with the dangerously high IQ, could really put himself down. He painted the walls of the renovated garage a striking green and trimmed them in refreshing white. Large rug remnants cushioned the floor. Uncle Ike shared the pulpit with Papa and two blind church elders sat on either side of the small church when William came forward to give his report. We settled in as he began.

"On Monday, I had Thoughtfulness Through a Good Deed. I did some diapers. I rated 40 percent."

"Help us, Jesus," Blind Mother Craton hollered.

"Tuesday, I had Humility Through Drudgery."

Backyard swimming pool.

Ruthie pinched me.

"I cleaned the toilet bowl."

"All right," Papa said.

"Eeenh!" Uncle Ike said.

"Help us, Jesus," Mother Craton hollered.

"I rated 60 percent."

Ruthie winked at me.

"On Wednesday," William continued, "I had Special Sacrifice. I gave up sweets and meats."

"Help us Jesus."

"I rated 75 percent."

"All right."

"Eeenh!"

"Thursday, I did my resolutions which are to think of God more each day, to practice my instrument more each day, and to be a better Christian."

"Help us, Jesus."

"I rated 20 percent."

"The truth shall set you free," Mother Craton called.

Papa gave William the eye.

Uncle Ike said, "Eeenh."

"I ask you to pray for me," Brother William said, then took his seat.

"I shall read my schedule for the past week," Valerie said in a sweet smooth voice. She had large eyes and dimples. Soft hair and smooth black skin. Smiles touched Mother Craton's lips and Brother Simpson's lips. They could feel her beauty in her voice. They listened.

"Six o'clock, rise. Six o'one, pray. Six o'two, make bed. Six o'three, brush teeth. Six o'four, breakfast, no I mean wash. Wash." I would never see another schedule so tight as hers until reading Booker T. Washington's *Up from Slavery*.

"I rated 90 percent," Valerie finally concluded.

James barely had a chance to come forward, he barely addressed us before Papa cut in.

"Let's hear it son. You been awfully bad last week."

James's facial expression changed; he'd adjust his ratings, bringing them down so that he wouldn't further anger his father, a father not fully aware that he put too much pressure on this son.

LausDeo was only visiting that day, having joined the Air Force, and spoke casually as he stood before us. "I don't have a written report," he explained.

"Help us, Jesus."

"But I must say that I have been striving . . ."

Papa watched him closely, this son who took up drinking in the armed services. This son who had taken up the sword.

"And I have been . . ." Deo fingered his shaven upper lip, "I have been," he repeated, then collected himself, his voice suddenly brimming with energy, "pressing toward the mark!"

"Well I do say," Papa said.

"Mercy, Jesus," Mother Craton called.

"And for my testimony, I'll sing 'It's Been a Great Change.'" And he did sing, weight resting on one foot, the other foot forward. This first brother who never struck me in my girlhood years, who bought for my thirteenth birthday a subscription to *Writers Digest*, who would steer me away from casual men until I had a clearer sight of the world around me. His voice was not so full volumed, but lazy, low and deep.

Oldest brother, LausDeo.

> The way I use to walk
> I don't walk no more.
> It's been a great change since I been born.

Then came the Tuesday morning when I stopped at Queens General Hospital to ask for a visitor's pass, and two young girls chewing gum said, "She's dead," meaning my mother. Two years after the birth of her fifteenth, Melie Dike, dead. An older woman found me bent over crying on the hospital grounds and said what happened. And said keep yourself together. That she was sorry. How old was your mother?

"Forty-five."

"She was a young woman. Just hold yourself up."

"Yes ma'am," I said.

"Just hold yourself up."

Back home, I watched through the screen door as Papa rolled his bicycle to a stop. He parked beneath the grape arbor and came into the house.

"Mamma died this morning, sir."

"She did?"

"Yes sir."

He took a deep breath and headed for the door.

"I'll go with you," I said.

"You will?"

"Yes sir."

At the hospital, the Indian doctor said we did everything we could. She died of cancer of the pancreas. We would like to perform an autopsy, he said.

"No," Papa said. "I think she's been cut enough."

"You'll be helping others."

"No," Papa said again. Because they had cut her bone days ago without his permission. They cut the bone and stained the arm red, but never explained why.

"We came to see the body," I said.

We walked down concrete paths past many buildings, way out to the morgue. It seemed a long journey with several turns. We stepped into a little booth-sized room to take refuge, to ask directions. Behind the desk a matronly blonde in white paused considerably to hear us. Spread before her at many angles were several dozen cards stamped death. Death. Death. And so many more to stamp. More than a hundred, newly dead. She gave directions and we found the morgue. We stood together facing a small window, father and daughter. We could see several covered stretchers, but the attendant went further back and came rolling my mother. He pushed the stretcher close to the window, pulled back the sheet and through the window flashed the hundred dreams I could not remember. For almost a year I awoke to find my pillow soaking wet. I had spent the night crying, but lifting my head in the morning, I could not remember why. Now, the shining glass. The small window. My mother's face, the perfect teeth stained yellow. The facial muscles strained in the final fight with death. I had looked through this window night after night in a hundred dreams. A year before she died, I had seen my mother's fragile golden umbra blasted to a red eternity.

"She's dead, all right," Papa said.

I was twenty-two. The youngest, Melie, was two. Please take good care of the baby, Grandmother (paternal) wrote me. My dear granddaughter, you have to be the mother for them now. You will be a good little mother to them for you was always good to them so you will be good to them now because this is the time to do the same thing. And she enclosed two dollars instructing me to buy them candy.

My girlhood was over, the years gone when I pumped my weight against the playground swings until they flew breathlessly high. Gone.

I stayed close to home, that first autumn, making beds, cooking, getting the children off to school. My eyes stayed wet. My eyes seemed to steam continuously, all on their own. Throughout the city, my sisters and brothers were in schools, crying. By December I was resisting Papa who didn't want me to go to work. He prayed over me. But in January 1966 I was a caseworker for the City of New York. I had a mother all my growing years. I had a card from my mother, a handmade card to mark my graduation from college. I wanted money in my pocket to buy new shoes for them the way Grandmother had bought new shoes for Ruthie and for me.

Grandmother's letter gave me courage. But I knew there was no substitute for a mother. Your mother is larger than the April sun. You snuggle close to her solid belly when the gusting wind blows. Her voice is peaceful as long shadows on rainy days. She is more than magic, your mother. You stretch her body walls to force your way into life. You make her scream, yet she smiles and cries when she sees your tiny face. Her laughter is like the surface of a swift flowing river. She makes the morning spill in long straight lines. There is no substitute for your mother. The earthy smells of your mother's legs, her oiled hands against your face and head. Her voice fills the tiniest corpuscles of your body. She smells like the sun. You learn her soft acrid stench in the toilet, inhale her sweet salt smells after a bath. Her voice is like paper shades on tight springs zipping up to let in sudden floods of winter sun. Her slippered footsteps, her winter glance pricks a thousand-year-old memory. Her rapid supple fingers at the piano make you laugh. Feel her body warm and solid, resting against you as she examines your school compositions.

"Why did you come to visit?" elementary school teachers asked me, surprised that a sister would think to visit her siblings' classes.

Because my mother did, I could have said. "Because I had the day off" is what I said.

The first two years after Mamma's death, Papa decreed no family celebrations. But in the third year, we celebrated Father's Day. After all, he was our one parent now. He was our joy and our grief. We couldn't wait to get at him. He aided us by insisting that we give anonymously. We had all written our cards, some more than one, all cards unsigned. That Sunday morning, downstairs, we waited for him. The parakeet, Pickle, perched on the kitchen faucet, whistled and chirped until Melie the youngest, now five years old, cupped his hands under the cold running water; the bird jumped in and lifted one wing and let water roll over and under it. He seemed so human, Melie so maternal. The bird carefully clutched Melie's fingers and turned to wash the other wing. Then finally he jumped from Melie's hands and shook, flinging water, too heavy to fly. The feathers soon fluffed full and dry and the bird perched on Melie's finger.

But before Melie got the bird into his cage, the bedroom door upstairs opened.

"He's coming!"

It closed.

We measured Papa's movement down the steps, his rapid walk down the hall toward the dining room, and when his face hit the doorway, we shouted, "Happy Father's Day." It was a roaring noise of twelve trained voices.

"Well," Papa paused surveying our faces, the decorations, flowers, fruit, cake, wrapped presents and cards. "Is this Father's Day?"

The youngest brothers were scandalized.

"I didn't know this was Father's Day."

Melie suddenly stopped smiling, and the bird flew to Papa's head as he read aloud the sign strung across the room, "Happy Father's Day . . . it must be. Well, let's get on with it."

He sat in his favorite chair, put his eyeglasses on with the parakeet standing on his bald spot, peering over his thick graying eyebrows. How to get that bird off my father's head!

"O, let him stay there," Papa said. "He thinks that's his spot."

We relaxed, relieved.

It was a good fifteen minutes before Papa read nineteen of the twenty cards, all arranged in effective sequence, several making fun of his balding head, others suggesting that he a teetotaler celebrate with a drink. The final card was Naomi's.

The card asked, "Are you a father?"

Papa looked at us.

"Keep reading," I prompted.

"Please answer the following questions. One. Do you have a bald spot?"

The younger children laughed raucously and the bird chuckled in his parakeet voice.

"Two. Do you preach? Three. Do you cook the Sunday dinner?"

"Yes you do!" Melie reminded him.

"Four. Are there a lot of eyes looking at you?" Papa glanced around and found twelve sets of dark eyes trained directly on him. He shook his head, and filled the room with a ripping laughter.

"Five," he continued, still laughing. "Five. Are you surrounded by several heads shaped exactly like your head?" The house dissolved in noise. "Then . . . then congratulations. You *are* a father. This *is* your day. Happy Father's Day."

The fourth Sunday would become my day, Poetry Sunday. In the afternoon service I would teach what I had been taught in college. Hyperboles, oxymorons, apostrophes, metaphors.

"How fast would you like to run?" I asked on a fourth Sunday of the month.

"Fast as lightning," Melie said.

"I'd like the rhythm of my feet to be as fast as the drums I beat," Earthel, the eleventh, said.

"That's fast," Uncle Ike said.

"I'd like to run as easy as a boat floats," William the brilliant, the seventh, said.

"As fast as the heart responds to danger, love and joy," Ruthie, the sixth, said.

That was fast. The world was waiting, the South and the West, Egypt and Nigeria. I had been holding several chapters of a novel in progress. Days of regret and days of satisfaction lay ahead. Before too late, I needed to record my heart's response to danger, love and joy.

A SECRET YOU CAN'T BREAK FREE

DAVE SMITH

I am old enough now to realize we are all trying to live sufficiently long to see the self come true. None of us is likely to make it. Therefore we invent selves, we prance and pose and dream and labor, confirming what we might be by what others think we are and by what we see we have been. The pictures a family takes of itself, of its members, are only the images of its dream selves. But that dreaming is the truth of the family as sure as the stories given from generation to generation. The truth, we like to think, is sweet and sustaining. It may be. Or may not.

The Way

I stand in front of the garage my grandfather built with his own hands, his lesson to the family in all things: self-reliance. The interior behind me is empty now and dark. I'm facing Buxton Avenue, in my tenth year, dressed up to go somewhere with the adults. It's high summer and sticky next to the swamp that borders my grandparents' house. I'm afraid of that dark garage but I love the swamp with its tide and banks of black mud where the thousands of holes of the fiddler crabs yawn. There's an iron poker holding the garage door open and I like to poke it into those holes to see what will come out. I try to open the holes wider in order to see into the darkness where, I imagine, so many are waiting to greet me.

But that mud can be bad. Once I sank to my waist and it felt like someone was pulling me when I tried to get away. Some older boys got me out before the tide came in. From where I was I could see my grandmother's back porch, the one that tripped her so she broke her arm. I saw the bone then. It was awful.

I'll come back to this house one day and it will be locked. The garage will yawn, startled as now, but nobody answers me. Then I'll find Mrs. Gee, who lives in the brown shingle house next door, who keeps (I've heard) a dead daughter upstairs, and she'll tell me my grandmother went to the hospital at the end of Buxton Avenue. I'll run all the way and find her. After I stop crying she'll let me look out her window at the water of Hampton Roads where the *Monitor* and the *Merrimac* fought. She says I make her afraid, wanting to stand down there when the hurricanes come, but I know she

Dave Smith

loves the storms, too. When she gets tired, I go home and wait for my grandfather because I know she won't die. Not this time.

During the winters I go back to my parents and to school and things turn serious. The only pictures of the family then are holidays, and there aren't many. But summers I live with my grandparents. Nana and I stay up late to listen to the Yankees cream the Orioles on the radio and she cooks me pancakes or French toast or anything I want, anytime. I play baseball at the playground and I ride my bike that's painted in big spots like a horse I saw in a movie. My father would kill me if he saw it. I crab and fish and swim. Nana gives me money to take the bus downtown and out to the Mariners Museum. I watch the boats and the paintings of boats until I can almost see them moving. I invent parts that I play, a sailor, a pirate, a Marine. Then later I tell Nana everything because she wants to know.

Nana is the Queen of the family. In the summer the mailman, the milkman, even the Jewel Tea man laugh with her. After school starts we only come to her house on holidays like Thanksgiving, Christmas, and Easter. She cooks for days and the little rooms fill up with people complaining they'll bust from eating. Then they sit around telling stories about the family, the men having drinks and laughing, one telling something on another one and that one adding to it, connecting to yet another one until we're all the way back to Lynchburg, Virginia, and our home place, the Silk Farm, and every now and again one of them will say "You better put this in your cap little buddy." Then I will say "Yessir, I will." I don't think I'd know a thing in the world if it wasn't for all the stuff they make me stick in my head. I even know names of cousins and neighbors and places I probably won't ever see. Nana says some I *shouldn't* see. Or know.

My mouth gets all wet just thinking about those days of ham, turkey, chicken, candied yams, white potatoes and gravy, string beans, fresh rolls and biscuits, creamed corn, cauliflower, beets, then pumpkin and cherry and apple pie, ice cream, and the strong coffee that I didn't drink of, only smelled. Suddenly I'd look around and everybody'd be asleep, just like they were all dead. The last one would be my grandfather, holding out somehow, then tipped over and snoring. My grandmother loved him very much. She'd come in and put a little pillow behind his head. Then, when he woke up, off he'd go to bed because he had to work early in the morning. Once she and I went to a movie and had to leave before it ended because she said she was afraid what might happen if she didn't have his dinner ready at five when he came home from work. I remember him at the head of the table, passing all the bowls to us. I used to try to imagine him scared, selling apples on corners during the Depression, like she said, with sick kids, but I never could. He was the smartest, strongest man I knew.

No one ever told me he played the trumpet, played it long and fine with notes too good for the smoky roadhouses up and down the hill shades of Maryland's mountains, but just right for Pittsburgh, say, or D.C. When I asked, they said "self-taught." He said nothing, only that he was young then. When I show him the picture, he says he remembers the shadow. At eighty-five, what will I remember?

Dave Smith

The Deer Slayers

It's cold when I wake, the crisp and forbidding cold of that stillest time of the morning to be, but I'm excited so I slide out of bed quickly, throwing back my grandmother's purple comforter. Already the house is full of the smell of frying bacon and eggs. I can taste the cinnamon toast. I take a little rug and place it over the grid of the floor furnace, then I stand on it so hot air blows up my pajama legs. While I drink my chocolate milk, I listen to Gramps thumping in his bedroom, getting ready. I wonder why they don't sleep in the same bed, like my parents, but I never ask.

When I climb in, the heater is running in his green Hudson, a color like the leaves when the sun presses through them. The seat is big as my own bed at home and prickly with its seatcover. In the trunk there's his long shotgun, my .22 rifle, and our lunches. I'm holding the thermos of coffee that always pours out extra sweet and is the exact shade of mud in the country lane where we'll stop. It won't be light then, not yet. Mr. Olson will be with us. He and Gramps will laugh all the way to the woods and then a shadow would make more noise. While they're talking, I will watch the dark and then the James River that we pass over on the way to Smithfield. The river is nothing but black and it doesn't scare me yet. In a few years, after my father is killed in an automobile accident not far from this bridge, I'll have a nightmare about driving to the top and finding the rest gone. I wake up when I hit the water. But the dream keeps coming back. It is not something I could talk to Gramps about.

My grandfather is the most precise man I have ever known. Sometimes I have realized with not a little pain that my life should have been his. I have liked school, learning and thinking. My grandfather hungered for education but was lucky to finish high school. He was glad in those hard times to get work on the B&O Railroad. He studied at night and then he was quickly promoted to foreman. He invented something like a coupling that every car in the world still uses. He gave it to the company—free!—because that was the kind of loyalty he had been raised to. I've seen that heritage in his father's eyes and those of his grandfather, Union Captain Asham Buckner. But soon enough the B&O uncoupled all grandfathers. Mine drove a truck, if he could find one, and sold apples, and got by in the Depression for two years, with one child bedridden and dying. Money might have helped. He thought education would.

He left the family. Went to Baltimore, got back on the railroad. Studied to be a draftsman, became one, studied at night at Johns Hopkins University. No degree, but he would become an engineer, a mustang, who developed wind tunnels for jet aircraft and before that ship-hull innovations and after that land transports for the U.S. Army. But first he paid back every cent he had borrowed during those two awful years and he learned denial. And he practiced it on the family. But he never stopped being what he always was, the family dreamer. He knew what flight would come to and is one of those who made it what it is now. His dreaming made him abandon the hills, where they said he'd be back. He wouldn't. After him, the family went looking for what it needed, in cars, all over the country, in planes and boats. It would grow worse, more rootless, with each generation.

We stand beside that rutted lane, off in the weeds a little. I'm shivering now because it's cold and we don't move and I watch stars that glimmer grandly so far off. A tall holly casts a dark shade, I think, even though it is still night. I imagine the world will always be like this, the darkness, the quiet, the burning flare of my grandfather's Camel when he puffs. He and Mr. Olson talk about where they'll be. Gramps tells Olson to return to the car at noon. Mr. Olson says "Ya, Harry!" In all the days I hunted with Gramps, he never once stayed in the woods past noon, his rule, never once gave in to the hunger for one more crack at a kill.

Before I know it we're up the side of a little ridge. It's pitch black as we heel away leaves in a circle. Then the ground is clear. We can stretch, stand silently, pee if we have to. Sometimes he'll smoke a Camel. If you pay attention to the wind and trees, he says, you know what will happen.

I have my .22 bullets in my hand, which is in my pocket. I shiver, even though I am wedged against him on the log. The woods are slowly turning blue and I think I probably could find the car, if I wanted to. The .22 rifle, once Uncle Harry's, lies unloaded across my lap. He'll show me what to shoot and when. His Model 12 Winchester pump lies across his knees, empty still of its three deer shells. Far away, then, the bump-bump of a shotgun. He loads quickly, and sits very still.

Hours pass as the sun spatters onto the canopy of hot-colored leaves. When the wind gusts, a shower of leaves shoots down through the gray trunks. Wind cuts over the ridge above us for a while, then dies. Gramps seems to know how to choose a good spot. But I'm tired and want to ask if it isn't time to go. I have already asked several times. If I ask again and he doesn't answer, I'll know he's angry. My grandmother said not to make him angry. Just when I don't think I can wait any longer, he nudges me. I look at him. He nods across the hollow. I don't see anything but gray trunks of hickories and colored leaves. Then I see the holly thicket like a wall of darkness. And out of that wall, stepping like an egret I have seen in the swamp, comes a deer. It walks straight toward us, as if it is magical, so sweet and beautiful. The head is high, with horns, the ears twitch, and the tail keeps flipping. Right at the moment the deer steps on the lane below us, my grandfather springs up and fires, pumps, fires, pumps, fires. The deer jumps, a kind of small, broken leap, as if he was tied to something that yanked him back. Then he lies in the leaves, almost invisible. I have to squint to see him, though I don't wear glasses for years yet.

As Mr. Olson and Gramps load the buck into the Hudson's trunk, I notice the eyes are glazed but open, a deep brown. Mr. Olson will take the deer and clean it and give us good cuts. We stand in the lane, sun high now, and Gramps pours us all steaming coffee. Then he pours whiskey into his cup and Mr. Olson's.

Over the James River, my grandfather stops talking to Mr. Olson and tells me "I'm sorry we forgot to shoot the .22, son. We'll do that next weekend." I tell him that's fine. It is. I had forgotten the rifle in my excitement. Now all I can think of is the deer, dead. The James River is a cold blue if you look close but farther off it is silver and white and very pretty. I can see oystermen working. The boats, far distant, look like black specks to be shaken from a clean tablecloth.

All I can think of is how quiet and beautiful it was in the woods with that circle where we whispered and the birds would come right up, then veer off. Then whammo! I didn't blame Gramps. I wanted to shoot, too. I even kept some of the leaves with spots of blood that dried black and held until years later the leaves crumbled away to nothing.

Foot Notes and Trees

Tiny, mean, shale-spirited people, my other side. Out of the dark veins, the chill grottoes, the snake-nested ledges of West Virginia: Ralph and Xena Mae, my father's parents. She snaps her words out, all five feet of her, props herself up with a pillow to see through, not above, the steering wheel. Then drives. He does not, ever. A ticketseller for the B&O railroad through four decades, my grandfather Smith inhabits a cage the size of a closet. When Xie Mae dies, he retires to the house and remains forever. I remember being taken there: car packed late, the dark drive, looking up at stars until sleep came, then my father banging the door to be let in. I'd wake in a strange, always cold room, sometimes my grandparents' room where the framed photograph of a naked lady hung over their bed. They would always be in the kitchen. They seem frightened and apt to bite, like little dogs.

Imagine, this house has been given to them! The car, too! Years back there had been another house and they had rented a room to a young railroad engineer from Paw Paw, West Virginia. Their home became his. He never married. We called him Uncle Melvin Holliday. Large, loud as the wind, a great joker, he made me sob when he told me he kept his best fishing worms in the apple sauce—but I had to eat it anyway. Weekends, while my parents visited old pals in Cumberland, he took me to fish the Potomac. I caught bass, walleye, pickerel, one rainbow. I also caught his cheek on one cast and watched him cut the hook out with his penknife while I held the hand-mirror. In his will, he left them the house. He left me a German Mauser rifle

with a hand-carved stock. No one else got anything. I hated him for his taunting, his loneliness, his diabetes, yet he was nearly the only thing human in that house.

The godawful bitterness of that house. Where does it come from? What happens when you let in a third member, an outsider, who becomes the keeper and provider? His bedroom was across the hall from theirs, a bigger, richer room. Not to be entered, I was told. He also had the room in the basement, rich with fishing gear, tools, guns, a million things to look at and through.

Down there once, in the dark and stinky place, my grandmother made me stand and pee in front of her because she had cleaned the upstairs bathroom. And once she made me sit all day in a chair by a window because her neighbor's grandson had come visiting from the country and all he wanted to do was stare quietly outside. She had a goldfish pond out back and beside it two carved headstones for her bulldogs. When my father was killed, they sent a card. Dull, bland, hopeless as the pipe smoke my grandfather left wherever he moved, a sourness in the air.

But not Melvin, enigma, booming through people's dreams with that big B&O diesel, not this womanless, warty broker of our tribe's destiny. In the kitchen his papery thighs would rest exposed under a thick blue robe while he tapped the needle free of bubbles and stuck it in and stuck it in, again, until you had to turn away. But he was the heartbeat there. Xena Mae was the flesh and giver of flesh. Therefore, I am. But what, alone on the tracks as they roared against all the walls of darkness, did they think of the world? Did any of them think?

The Shadow Knows

Tommy Dorsey. Glenn Miller. A handful of Gillette shaving lotion slapped on my childish cheeks. My father's house coming alive, my father going to work. The Friday night fights. *To look sharp, da-da-da-dada, to feel sharp da-da-da-dada!* Summers he was a walking odor, sweat and mildew. Penny loafers with bright copper pennies. Stacks of *Hot Rod* magazine, a cheap education worth everything to me now. The secrets of go-fast revealed. His fire-red 1932 Ford coupe, chopped and channeled, with a gleaming chrome tri-carburated 1951 Mercury flathead V-8. We had a little deuce coupe before the Beach Boys were born. His passion was cars, the American ache. I got it from him. From his aqua-blue and white 1955 Ford convertible and his 1957 lime and white Ford convertible. Then from the 1930 Model A he bought for me and sold for the 1949 two-door coupe we decked and frenched and lowered. Then from the white Alfa Romeo Guiletta Spider with red leather upholstery and the small mirror on the dash, no seat belts. That one killed him. May 5, 1960, Mother's Day. Age thirty-nine.

They called him "Jeddie" at Fort Hill High School, in Cumberland. He was an all-state guard in basketball, scoring two points his senior year. You can't play better defense than that. He had a thick, strong, hairy chest, legs that would get a good horse shot, and eyes as bad to see through as pond ice. There are almost no pictures of him with glasses. His vanity was consummate.

Early in the war he began volunteering. No luck. Too blind. He memorized the eye-chart, got inducted, having spent enough time hanging around with the guys who wore letter sweaters and whined. Having, the truth be known, moved to Portsmouth, Virginia, and commenced working for Kitty Cornwell's dad at the Naval Shipyard. Man it was a good life, cat's meow, parties at the beach, parties all over! Then he and Kitty got married. Then there was a son. Somewhere in all that, the U.S. Navy.

Basic training was routine for an athlete like him. But in advanced training somebody moved the goddamn boat just when he put his foot on the dock. He knew when the knee hit that it was bad. Kitty's brother Harry Jr. was on his way to the USS *Croatan*; Jeddie Smith was on his way to the knife, to a butcher who left him with a knee that would suddenly, years later, swell to the size of a basketball. They discharged him. He went back to the shipyard, took evening classes at the College of William and Mary, the University of Virginia, a stint at the Massachusetts Institute of Technology. Wound up a naval engineer, no degree, stuck in a fine job. He wanted to run a small pro shop for golfers but he had a terrible handicap. He had a family.

He casts no shadow in the photograph where he poses. How ludicrous he seems gazing provocatively skyward like a Viking, his right hand on the verge of a defensive fist, his left peaceful but poised for a deflection. The

knees of his dungarees (not *jeans*) compose his battle scars in defiance of regulations. You almost don't notice the handle of his service knife protruding from his rear pocket. Then you notice. He's twenty here, the salt water of an unknown Virginia cove spreading behind him, as it must have for John Smith and the others at Jamestown, a high glaring sun everywhere, the fleshy clouds like the promises from a girl. He might laugh at the Romantic posturing of this shot, if my son showed it to him, but he would like it, too, like what it declaims about all the boys who spilled down out of the ridges and sharp cleavages of rock to say to Hitler and Yamamoto and Il Duce what he never said in my presence: Fuck you! He was hard-nosed, as he would have said, and ready for the future. Except he would not get to the future.

Naturally, that's where I am.

Holding me in his arms, he hurts with glare. He can't even see the photographer. He's now the most responsible, most hard-working, most ambitious son-in-law that Kitty's dad has ever had. Also the only one. Tie, suit, overcoat. They rent my grandfather's spare apartment in Park View. They walk by the golf course in Glen Sheila (long gone), the boat harbor (no boats now), and the crab house (torn down). It is low tide and you can very nearly smell the rank mud, the dead fish, the scum of naval oil, and that crab-becoming-fertilizer always in the wind there. That's my grandfather's first boat in the rear. But who is that woman in black who seems to have ambled into the shot as casual as death?

What interests me is how little I know him.

He did not hunt, rarely fished. He preferred games of collision and speed. Once he whipped me for crying when our little league baseball team lost a game. Losing was terrible, acts of weakness were unforgivable. I began playing little league football at age seven. His praise came when the other kid didn't get up after a tackle. At sixteen I quit the high school team. I'd had enough of the August sweat and dirt in my teeth and 100-yard wind sprints and bull-in-the-ring games of tackle. I took my girlfriend to the game and wound up sitting behind him. He refused to speak to us. On Monday I was back with the team, demoted to third-string scrub, and I finished the season as starting center only because of my teammates' injuries. I don't believe he ever got over my quitting.

There are no drive-ins with jukeboxes anymore, no skating waitresses, no places to get together with the gang left. The town I grew up in—countryside, really—isn't there. It's wall-to-wall subdivisions, new roads, busing. My junior year in high school was the year of Virginia's "Massive Resistance" against integration. We were in the county. City kids, white ones, transferred to us. I don't know what the black ones did. In that darkness of the human heart, what did my father say to me? Nothing. He became the hole in my life. It seems he, like everything else from that time, was beginning to fade.

During my entire junior year he refused to speak to me, except to say the usual: Take the garbage out. Or, "No," when I asked for money. I stopped asking. I caddied, washed cars, mowed lawns, worked the supermarket. His life was sealed from mine, a seal broken only when he used his leather belt to beat my sister for lying. If he spoke to my mother, I don't recall it. Into that hole have gone all the people I grew up with, the fields I walked, the pond I swam in, the drive-ins, parties, movies, team practices, games, days and nights. The schools have been redistricted and rebuilt. Blacks are bused there: the whites moved farther out, then again. And yet, it is not a racial malice that threatens whatever life might still be there. It is the mall developers, the water polluters, the grubbers and greeders who have somehow dug our hole, then pushed us into it, and who finally keep widening it until we never get out. Then the garbage piles up until we act like garbage. You won't hear them say that at the Churchland Baptist Church where they know that masochism, like revenue, has its limits.

The church cemetery where we buried him had a crowd of smooth-faced stones, a little mossy, and a heritage of tall oaks. Honeysuckle walled you in.

You could smell a farmer's pigs nearby. You could hear the conversation of men spill out of Speers' Cafe.

I'd delivered my papers that mild Sunday morning and I was startled to hear him volunteer to take my mother to Nana's, though it was Mother's Day. I took my girl to an afternoon movie instead, Jerry Lewis on some kind of ship. The usher found us by shouting my name. I drove the 1949 coupe as fast as it would go, burning oil and plodding. The doctor met me at the emergency room. There had been an auto accident but my daddy was fine, going in surgery. Mother was upstairs and needed me for support. My vision of her came true: slashed skin, iodine swabbings, bandages, swelling. Barely conscious, sedated. Were others in that room? The doctor arrived suddenly: He was sorry. My father hadn't made it. I'm confused. Hadn't made what? The nurse explains but I refuse to believe he is dead, even though paroxysms of guilt begin. If I had only gone to Nana's. If I had been a better son. If. If.

I used to have a dream. In it, I knew my father was given a government spy assignment so secret we were told he was dead. But somehow I knew he would come back. After a while, he began to enter the dream. I'd open the door and there he would be, but he wouldn't come in. When I became a writer, I wrote about this often, always badly. The truth was that he went into shock because the doctor wasn't paying attention and an intern gave him a sedative. Not too many years later that doctor once again failed to remain alert and a jealous husband castrated him in the act. One more into the hole.

We're all gathered at the hole in the cemetery. There's a tent and rows of chairs and heaps of flowers. The sun is like liquid fire. Why isn't the hole stark, brutal, plain dirt? I don't remember anyone there or anything that happened. I remember the beautiful green place. Now the cemetery is lapped by concrete. There's a six-lane intersection and a 7-11 store next to it. The trees are gone. Malls surround the area as far as anyone can see. Without blue laws, it is never silent there. Texaco, McDonald's, K-Mart, Revco, all of them pumping, stuffing, sucking, eating. There is no live thing taller than a man's knee. There is only the hard flare of light all day and the neon darkness all night. The dead have to go deep in the hole to escape.

I was seventeen.

The Empress of Sterling Point

They were a family and she, my mother, came with them from that hard place where life was bitter, came to the shore of Virginia, as before in the old time and from places of great bitterness so many had come. Therefore, I was. Behind them the burrowings of coal and steel-melting heats; ahead something. Maybe. Her father, rough as a cob and stiff in his word, saw while he sat down to hunt the squirrels that the game went where food was. So he went. They followed and we, I, became a Virginian. But not all did. Uncle Lloyd, his brother, over six feet, blue eyes, a foreman of the roundhouse, the loveliest smile in Maryland, wanted to go. He wanted to raise his three children in that better place. Said the flame-haired sweetheart Aunt Dot: you'll have to go without us. Lloyd died of cancer that reduced him to less than 100 pounds of meat before he was fifty. My favorite. Also the favorite of my mother, Kitty.

Dave Smith

Could you resist falling in love with this young woman? You see her posed in City Park, hear the boogie-woogie on the portable radio, the joy on her face melts you. I swear it does. You can, if you like, take her into the Chevrolet behind her and take her dancing. They don't come any lighter on the feet. Did you ever see a dream walking? OK, she's sitting. Still, a dream, the future for whoever's taking this picture.

What kind of future? Class! She's got it. Brunette, medium height, sassy enough to win every contest she might enter, which isn't many because she thinks that sort of stuff is silly. But she's not anybody's princess yet. She's just Kitty Cornwell Smith, newly married American girl. I know the future that's ahead of her. It's the widening hole. She'll have to work sometimes, sometimes not. She'll hurt bad but she's tough and she'll make out OK.

One Sunday they fought, the shouting horrible and frightening, then she got in the car and left. Later my father put my sister and me in the second-hand Plymouth coupe and we drove for a while until we found a street on the edge of town, its houses small like garages. He honked and honked. Finally, she came out and they talked, hard and flat. There seemed to be someone hovering behind the screen door of the house. I could hear them speaking about divorce, the first time I heard the word, when I went to bed. It sounded like death to me.

We lived in Sterling Point, a colonial suburb where every house had colonial furniture and some had colonial dog houses. My father designed our house but my mother laid in the creaky antiques you couldn't sit on. We didn't have many fires in the fireplace because that meant dirt. This was on Bridges Avenue, the pine straw so thick it was like a brown carpet everywhere. I fished in the pond down the street, hiding from the owner. Across the street lived Mr. Cross who lost his leg to diabetes. Down a block was my friend Billy who got thrown from a car on his way back to college. The other way you could find several girls who were not particular what you did to them or when. Our neighbor in the rear had a bad nervous breakdown. To the side, there was a pregnant daughter and a drop-dead heart attack. In the suburbs your lawn is your domain. Don't cross this, say the fences, flowerbeds, shrubs, trees, and everybody lives within the covenants of his cube of space. I delivered their papers, cut their yards, chased their daughters, played ball and fought with their sons, yet we were nothing to each other. When I left, I knew, I would never go back. But I thought the Empress would be there always.

Badly injured in the accident that killed my father, my mother felt marred and unvaluable. She accumulated insurance money. She began dating a jet pilot from Langley Air Force Base. He offered me a drink the first time I met him and I had never touched the stuff, so I offered to punch him in the mouth. Mother told me, in private, a cock-and-bull story about pilots facing death every time they go up, therefore needing to drink when they came down. I'm still amazed that at seventeen I knew where the story came from and why but she didn't. Then one day she married the Captain and he moved in. My memory started to unravel like the banks of a carefully dug hole and I can't recover much of those months.

In the fall of 1961 I found my way, alone, to the University of Virginia. At Christmas I went home with fellow students, all of us a little drunk, and arrived before my house in Sterling Point. I knocked on the door, finding it locked. A man I'd never seen asked what I wanted. Startled, I told him I lived there. He denied this, said he lived there. We danced back and forth with assertions and denials until, my panic growing, he said: Oh, you're the son of the woman who sold us the house.

But where would the Empress have gone? I drove my gold, D-stock, very fast 1958 Chevrolet Impala to my grandparents' house, watching the speedometer reach for 115 and then back off for curves. Because my grandfather admired the design of my father's house, he had built a duplicate for himself. Yet what a difference! In that house was no chronic despair, no constant verbal sniping, no gloomy silence, no festering angers. They met me in the yard, answering what I didn't even have to ask. She and the Captain had gone to Florida. She hadn't been able to face me about the sale.

When she finally divorced the Captain she had none of the insurance money. What she had she used to help me in school. I got loans, I worked. What she did and how she managed, I don't know. Things got hard for her. She went out with the Sheriff, whom I expected her to marry. She was far down but coming up when I saw her one night at my grandfather's. She had piled everything she owned now in a beat-up Plymouth Valiant and she was heading out. Under the yellow antibug light, I kissed her good-bye while moths fluttered like tiny servants. If you had seen her at one of the old drive-in burger joints, you'd keep going around slowly, hoping she'd notice.

What must it feel like to be knockout beautiful, widowed and under forty, well-off and then busted, adrift from your children and family, no friends who want you around their husbands, no job, no home, no money, and no future you can lay hands on? Is it worse if you're proud, intelligent, and terrified? When I try to think about her driving off into that night, I have to make my mind look somewhere else.

Tenderness and toughness are inexplicably mixed up in people I admire. Few of us are what we think—we're always more or less. Whatever the Truth is, it is parts of something, of the family. But the parts keep changing, swapping jobs and places, turning tough or tender when you expect the opposite.

They do what they do because of some act or acts that are so far back behind our memory that the oldest, crankiest one of us can't patch together what happened or why. Yet it's almost a rule that the elders have to keep telling us our story of the truth. They just don't have to tell it in any particular way. They can invent, like writers. They can bury it in a web of lies. There's also no rule about anyone having to understand. Our only rule is that we must look and listen.

I know men a little, enough, and it's no trouble to see them turning to her that night, other nights: high heels, slim ankles, tight waist, hair with a bit of acetylene in it, eyes that nail you to the wall, a voice that wouldn't hesitate to tell God to keep his hands to himself. So I understand the Sheriff, then the Mexican, then some who might have been generals or golf pros, all a little tacky with danger, none big-time. Then the Major, devoted to her, unwilling to let her buy groceries without him. So now she was the Empress again, buy it all, live right, yacht and house and golf course. After a while it was easy to forget driving off that night, the Captain, the loneliness, the hole that she found inside herself.

Don't wait, do. That's how an Empress thinks.

They went into business. As best I can tell it was the worst time for loans, for small businessmen, and they didn't know diddly about that world. They shot it all in less than two years, a big dream shattered like a good glass. But maybe there's something in what Nana used to call "quality folks" who can get hurt, sick, beaten by life, and still come back. These folks aren't picture-perfect but by God they live!

You don't get to be an Empress by sitting on your fanny. You have to get out and strut some. Sometimes I think of Aunt Dot waiting under that dark and coal-smelly roof where Uncle Lloyd died, her already old and crusty as a slice of unsold bread but safe with her three kids locally employed. Then I think of my mother hitting the honky-tonks and clubs, moving on up, and the Major splashing tips around while the ferrets are cutting his credit cards off. You can be an Empress if you have grit and style. But maybe that isn't enough. Maybe you also need all the kinds of love there are and each one just a little raggedy-edged like the top of an opened tin can. Everybody knows how quick and bad a can is to cut, how long you remember that particular soreness. But you go on and you eat and it isn't ordinary food anymore.

The Queen is Dead

She couldn't get her breath, that's how it started. Then some smart young doctor gave her the thing like a little stove pipe to breath on, or in. Soon enough she was down there at Riverside Hospital, grinning the way she did when you came in the room, a soap always on the TV, candy and flowers piling up. We thought it was fat, because she had plenty of the pounds. The doctors said they had some trouble regulating her blackouts and then they told us to take her home. They never said the blackouts were times she died and the Intensive Care nurses brought her back. They never told us about the chemicals and the electric shocks.

She was hunched up in the sofa corner right there in the den that had been my bedroom that year I was out of college and teaching high school and not making enough money to do more than handle the car payment. The afghan she made curled around her because she was shivering. My wife and I didn't talk so much as we played back all the gossip we could think of. My grandmother loved gossip just so long as it wasn't dirty. She never said a word to hurt another soul and I don't recall anyone saying one against her. The worst kind of disapproval I'd ever seen her show was the little word that

A Secret You Can't Break Free

sounded like "Oh" and the look that came with it. It might have been re-served for a small, dead, wormy thing you shoved under her nose. I don't mean she had no force. Lord, that woman had waded through a family of sicknesses, divorces, new marriages, lost children, poverty, wars, and enough nastiness to engender civil chaos. She kept us together in the family and she kept us apart, as was necessary. We all thought she'd live forever.

I wasn't married for long at that time. If it hadn't been for my grand-mother, I wouldn't have gotten married. I didn't want to and my wife didn't want to wait. You can see what that was leading to. My grandmother kept talking to us. Then she gave us the bed we slept on, the chairs and kitchen table, the linens and dishes, even the knives and forks. All used and tucked away. My mother was off wandering the world. My wife's folks declared we were alien and practiced silence on us. It was not a comfortable world. When it fell out that an old friend called and suggested I come to graduate school in the Midwest, a thing that had never once occurred to me, my wife and I thought twice and said fine. This particular night we went to see my grand-mother because we were flying out early the next morning to find a place to live. Also because she asked me to come see her.

August nights in Virginia make you feel like you're wearing a diver's wet suit. Sweat is a natural condition; breathing is not. The air resembles smoke. We left my grandmother's early, went to bed right away, hoped we might sleep. But we lived beside the river. Frogs, birds, horses in near fields, C-130s returning to Langley Air Field, even a house party upstream, all had noises to make. Somehow we fell asleep. Then the telephone rang. Even today the telephone can sting me with devastating fear.

I don't remember who called. Maybe it was my mother. I had just kissed my grandmother's cold cheek. I said I'd come back and tell her about the Midwest.

The rescue squad couldn't make it fast enough. She was dead when my grandfather checked her after the news. Sixty-three years of heartbeats.

We went flying up the dirt road from our house, through the new suburban ranchers. It was pitch black, about five, but at the lane's end everything was red and yellow bright. Fire woofed where a roof had been on a rancher. I stopped and stood in the yard and yelled, afraid there might be people in there. But, hell, anybody in there was long gone. I backed up from the heat and then somebody put a hand on my shoulder. Scared the fool out of me. Neighbor said the wife and the kids were out of town. Said the husband done it. Said she left him and he told her if she ever done that he'd just burn the son of a bitch down and he did. I could hear the sirens off in the darkness while I drove away. I knew they wouldn't do a damn bit of good. I knew that he knew it as well, that knife of a man standing just beyond the wall of the dark while he watched his life break and slide away with the sparks. If I am ever tempted to burn my house down, and I have been of that mind, I think it would mean what my grandmother's death meant. You take away your Queen and the family goes to hell in a hatbox.

Maybe my grandfather should have hired a lawyer and had him conduct a sort of town meeting where all the survivors get to bid on the furniture, pictures, clothes, and even vote on what the old man might do. Put aside the fact that her good will and love have got barely cold and the fact that he has a right to do only what his soul and long nights find agreeable. They could lay out benefits for him and conditions. Maybe my people thought that was their duty. But he was of another mind. My grandfather was the one about whom my grandmother would invariably say "He means well." She was right, too, but she was gone. Families are supposed to have a long memory, especially Southern families, but when it wants to that memory will shrink up like your nuts on a cold day.

So my wife and I went away to school. We had the kids, got jobs, dreamed our dreams, fattened and said our clothes were shrinking, and forgot the hole for a while. I mean the hole death leaves. Her folks talked to her in time. My grandfather remarried and my mother stopped talking to him. Later on my uncle's kids, having gone from puberty to adulthood without knowing him because of divorce, called him up and laughed. My best friend in high school got Hodgkin's disease and beat it. Two graduate students I worked with jumped to their deaths. Once there's no Queen to call the family together, to cut the pumpkin pie and pour the coffee, the hole is always close. I don't know what other people do to ward it off, to keep trying to fill it up, but I write poems and stories.

Go-Round, Go-Round

So many memories, and all of them so sweet with that mild weather of great joy, because it is just before the first coming of pain in the body and before the incomprehensible puzzlement of the heart as it breaks, and in each of them is the hard acorn of a secret you can't break free even with your father's old jack, the mysterious unknown that's the sound of voices with words you will not ever quite make out or the shift of a silk dress, navy blue with dots, when she has seen you coming. The thing remembered. The thing not known. The piece that is missing, gone into the hole of the past and the hole of death.

From the darkness, all that the light has seems to radiate with inner glow.

From the light, you can see almost nothing, squinting.

That kitchen where the grown-ups gather, how can it hold all that bursting forth of laughter and hugging and kissing?

In the garage there is the blue-green flame of the welding torch that turns the darkness harder, more obsessive, but you have been told not to look. It will hurt. It will blind hurt you.

When the fire went through the darkness gathered around that house, there was someone watching you, you knew this. It was not him. Her. She understood what was going to happen, summoned you, watched, was here, then, as you drove at the darkness, was in that fire-flaring light, going somewhere without you, climbing out of the hole.

Over the stenchy mud-flats with the tide out came the sun, came like a round face gliding over the crib, the bed, the life, and was looking at you. Love. It would take you in a big green car to the soapy surf of Buckrow

Beach and sit on the moonlit fenders while you swam, all alone as if you owned that eternity, and it would close the doors late, turn off the television, rise in the darkness to see you had your medicine. It would have a toe that twitched under the blanket, scars on the arm and belly and leg. It would keep trying to tell you all that it could not tell you, what you had to know, looking grimmer and older and more like the parched dirt in every photograph.

For them, the talk was not of the Truth. It was of the weaving of things, wishes and lies and dreams and lives, those past and to come.

There would be the seductive warp of hot food summoning all from the rooms of the houses, the quiet susurrus of sleepers, the tales of how we had all tried to climb the slopes we had been given.

Then we weren't looking in anymore. We were inside, watching our sons and daughters in their hunger to know. Sometimes we would lower our voices, sometimes not. We would try to tell them our stories.

CONTRIBUTORS

Sheila Bosworth was born in New Orleans in 1950. She received a B.A. from Sophie Newcomb College of Tulane University. In 1984 her first novel, *Almost Innocent*, was published; she is at work on a second novel, *Slow Poison*. Ms. Bosworth lives now in Covington, Louisiana, with her husband, a New Orleans lawyer, and their two daughters.

Robb Forman Dew was born in Mount Vernon, Ohio, in 1946. Four years later her family moved to Baton Rouge, Louisiana, where her father set up his practice as a neurosurgeon. She was married in 1968, to Charles Burgess Dew, and they have two sons, Stephen, born in 1971, and Jack, born in 1973. She began writing in her late twenties, and her first fiction was accepted for publication by the *Southern Review* on her thirtieth birthday, in 1976. She published her first novel, *Dale Loves Sophie to Death*, in 1981, and her second novel, *The Time of Her Life*, in 1984. She was the recipient of the American Book Award for the Best First Novel in 1982, and of a Guggenheim Fellowship in the same year. Her husband is the chairman of the History Department of Williams College, and they live in Williamstown, Massachusetts, with their two children.

Barry Hannah was born in Meridian, Mississippi, in 1942. His early home was in Forest, Mississippi, in Scott County. When he was young, his family moved to Pascagoula and then to Clinton, where he grew up. Hannah received a B.A. from Mississippi College and an M.F.A. from the University of Arkansas. He has been writer-in-residence at Clemson University, Middlebury College, the University of Alabama, the University of Iowa, the University of Montana, and Memphis State University; he currently holds that position at the University of Mississippi. His first novel, *Geronimo Rex* (1972), won a William Faulkner Prize. A second novel, *Nightwatchmen* (1973), was followed by *Airships*, a collection of short stories, which won the Arnold Gingrich Short Fiction Award. Hannah's most recent novels are *Ray* and *Tennis Handsome*. He is currently working on a new novel, *Hey, Jack!* Hannah has been honored by the American Academy of Arts and Letters and has received, among his many honors, a Guggenheim Fellowship.

Contributors

Josephine Humphreys was born in 1945 in Charleston, South Carolina, and graduated from Duke University, where she studied writing with Reynolds Price and William Blackburn. Her novel *Dreams of Sleep* won the 1985 Ernest Hemingway Foundation Award for outstanding first fiction, and she was awarded a Guggenheim Fellowship in 1986. Her second novel, *Rich in Love*, will be published in 1987. Married and the mother of two sons, she lives in Charleston, South Carolina.

James Alan McPherson was born in Savannah, Georgia, in September 1943. He grew up there, attended Morris Brown College in Atlanta, Georgia, Morgan State College in Baltimore, the Harvard Law School in Cambridge, Massachusetts, and the Writers Workshop at the University of Iowa. He has published three books: *Hue and Cry* (1969), *Railroad* (1976), and *Elbow Room* (1977). McPherson has also written a number of articles. His awards include a Pulitzer Prize (1979) and a fellowship from the MacArthur Foundation (1981). He is currently at work on some fiction.

Bobbie Ann Mason was born in Mayfield, Kentucky, in 1940. Her collection of stories, *Shiloh and Other Stories*, was nominated for the PEN/Faulkner Award for Fiction, a National Book Critics Circle Award, and an American Book Award; it received the Ernest Hemingway Foundation Award for the most distinguished first-published fic-

tion in 1982. Her novel *In Country* was published in 1985. She has received grants from the National Endowment for the Arts and the Pennsylvania Council on the Arts, as well as a Guggenheim Fellowship. Her stories have appeared in the *New Yorker*, the *Atlantic*, the *North American Review*, the *Paris Review*, *Mother Jones*, and other magazines. She is a contributor to "The Talk of the Town" in the *New Yorker*. She grew up in Kentucky and moved to the Northeast after graduating from the University of Kentucky. She now lives in Pennsylvania.

T. R. Pearson was born in 1956 in Winston-Salem, North Carolina. He is the author of the novels *A Short History of a Small Place*, *Off for the Sweet Hereafter*, and *The Last of How It Was*.

Padgett Powell was born in 1952 in Gainesville, Florida. He is the author of the novels *Edisto* and *A Woman Named Drown*. In 1986 he received a Whiting Foundation Writers' Award. He currently teaches writing at the University of Florida.

Dave Smith was born in 1942 and raised in Churchland, Virginia, in the Tidewater area, and now lives in Richmond, where in 1986 he was named Distinguished University Scholar by Virginia Commonwealth University. A professor of American literature at VCU, he has also taught at the University of Florida, the State University of New York at Binghamton, and the

University of Utah. In recognition of his writing he has received two National Endowment for the Arts fellowships in Poetry, a Guggenheim Fellowship, and an award for excellence from the American Academy and Institute of Arts and Letters. Among his books are *The Roundhouse Voices: Selected and New Poems* (1985), *Local Assays: On Contemporary American Poetry* (1985), *Southern Delights* (stories, 1984), and *Onliness* (a novel, 1981).

Ellease Southerland, born in 1943 in Brooklyn, New York, is the author of a novel, *Let the Lion Eat Straw*, which has been issued in Japanese and other international editions. In addition to lecturing at libraries and universities, she has taught literature of African peoples for fifteen years and is currently poet-in-residence at Pace University. Ms. Southerland is now at work on another novel, *A Feast of Fools*.

Al Young was born in 1939 in Ocean Springs, Mississippi. He grew up in the Magnolia State and in Detroit. Educated at the University of Michigan and the University of California at Berkeley to be a Spanish teacher, he began to publish stories, articles, and poetry in newspapers, music magazines, and literary journals while still in his teens. Since 1961 his homebase has been the San Francisco Bay Area. An active and prolific writer, Young's works include the novels *Snakes, Who is Angelina?, Sitting Pretty, Ask Me Now,* and *Seduction by Light*; several books of poetry, *Dancing, The Song Turning Back into Itself, Geography of the Near Past, The Blues Don't Change: New and Selected Poems, 22 Moon Poems,* and *Heaven: Collected Poems, 1958–1988*; two collections of essays, *Bodies & Soul* and *Kinds of Blue*; screenplays for Richard Pryor, Sidney Poitier, and Bill Cosby; and innumerable prose pieces for magazines. With the poet-novelist Ishmael Reed, Young is copublisher of the multicultural literary journal *Quilt*. Al Young's writing has been honored with many awards; moreover, he has been a Guggenheim Fellow, a National Endowment for the Arts Fellow, Mellon Distinguished Professor of Humanities at Rice University, and, most recently, a Fulbright Fellow in Yugoslavia.